PERSUASION TECHNIQUES

HOW TO ANALYZE AND INFLUENCE PEOPLE USING MIND CONTROL, ADVANCED MANIPULATION METHODS AND DARK PSYCHOLOGY

professional advice. The content within this book has been derived from various sources. Please consult a licensed professional before attempting any techniques outlined in this book.

By reading this document, the reader agrees that under no circumstances is the author responsible for any losses, direct or indirect, which are incurred as a result of the use of information contained within this document, including, but not limited to, — errors, omissions, or inaccuracies.

Table of Contents

Introduction

In our modern world, we rely the most on the use of persuasive tactics or techniques. Their strength depends on our ability to evaluate a situation and to choose the right weapons. Different psychologists have given different lists of basic tactics: these ones are offered to help you get a clear view in order to plan your influence strategy.

1. *Persuade Only Those Who Can Be Persuaded*

We can all be influenced at one time or another, provided the timing and the context is right. However, for some people, it can take a lot of persuading. Take a look at the politicians and their campaigns - they focus their money and their time almost exclusively on the small percentage of voters who are responsible for determining the outcome of an election. The very first step to successful persuasion is to identify and focus on the people who can, at that moment in time, be persuaded to follow you and your point of view. By doing this, a certain percentage of others - those who can't be persuaded at that moment in time - will be influenced later on to change their course.

2. *Get Your Timing and Content Right*

These are the building blocks of persuasion. Context is what provides a standard for what is and isn't acceptable. For example, an experiment carried out on Stanford prisoners showed that students who overachieve could easily be molded into prison guards with a dictatorial nature. The timing is what dictates what we are looking for from other people and from life. Often, when we marry, it is to someone very different to whom we may have been dating in our younger years, simply because what we want at any given time is subject to change.

3. *Uninterested People Cannot Be Persuaded*

You simply can't convince people to do something if they genuinely are not interested in what you have to say. In general, the human race is concerned primarily with their own individual selves and most of their time is spent thinking about three things – health, love, and money. The very first step to persuading someone is to learn to talk to that person about themselves. Appeal to their self-interest and you have their attention.

Continue to do it, and you will hold their attention for long enough to persuade them.

4. *Reciprocity is Compelling*

Whether we like it or not, most of the time that someone does something for you, you feel innately compelled to return the favor. It's the way we are made, a survival instinct that goes back many millions of years. You can use that reciprocity to your advantage by giving someone something they want; you can then ask for something much more valuable back from them, and they will feel compelled to do it. The principle of reciprocation is more effective if you are the first one to give and if your gift is personal and unexpected.

5. *Be Persistent but not Overbearing*

If you are prepared to keep on asking for what you want, to continue demonstrating real value, you will ultimately succeed in the art of persuasion. Take a wander back through history and look at the vast numbers of figures who have persuaded people through persistence, in both message and endeavor.

Look at Abraham Lincoln, look at what he lost – three sons, his mother, his girlfriend, one of his sisters. He failed abysmally in business, and he also lost at no less than 8 elections.

Still, his persistence paid off when he was finally elected as President of the Unties States. He never gave up and neither should you.

6. *Be Sincere in Your Compliments*

Whether we admit it or not, compliments do have a positive effect on us, and we are much more likely to place our trust in a person who is sincere and who makes us feel good. Try it – be sincere when you compliment a person, pay them compliments for something that they honestly wouldn't expect it to. Compliment them on something they had to work for: it can be something as simple as their clothing choice. Don't compliment them on their beauty or on other things they were born with. It's quite easy once you learn how to do it, and it costs nothing. The rewards will speak for themselves.

7. Set Your Expectations

One of the biggest parts to persuasion is learning to manage the expectations of others when it comes to placing trust in you and your judgment. If a CEO were to promise his employees a pay increase of 20% and then give them 30%, he would be rewarded much more than the CEO who promised 20% and only delivered 10%.

Learn to understand what other people expect of you and then over deliver on it.

8. Never Assume

This is a bad mistake to make: to assume what people are looking for. Instead, offer them your value. Take the sales world; often products and services are held back because it is assumed that people simply don't have the money to purchase them, or they have no interest in them.

Be bold, get out there and say what you have to offer, say what you can do for them and leave the choice to them. Be persistent, and it will pay off.

9. Make Things Scarce

Virtually everything has a value these days, on a relative scale.

We need the bare necessities to survive, so they have a far higher value than something we don't need. Often we want something because someone else has it. If you want to persuade people to want what you are offering, it may not be enough to point out the benefits of things or services we are offering. It could be much more effective if we would tell people about its uniqueness and what they could lose. That would create a scarcity feeling, and the less there is, the more people want it. The logic of scarcity is very simple: when something becomes scarce, people want it more.

10. Create a Sense of Urgency

One of the finer points of persuasion is being able to instill such a sense of urgency in people that they simply have to act straight away or miss out. If a person doesn't have any real motivation to want something now, they aren't likely to want it later on down the line either.

It's down to you to persuade them that time is running out; persuade them now or lose them forever.

11. Images are Important

Most people respond better to something they can see. Quite simply if they can see it, then it's real; if you just talk about it, then it might not even exist. Images are potent, and pictures really do speak a thousand words. You don't actually have to use images, just learn how to paint that image in a person's mind.

12. Truth-Tell

Sometimes, hard though it may be, the easiest way to persuade a person to trust you is to tell them something that no one else will say, something about themselves. Facing up to the truth is often the most meaningful thing any of us will go through. Do it without any judgment and without an agenda, and you will be surprised at how quickly that person responds favorably to you.

13. Build Up a Rapport

The human race is a funny thing. We tend to like those who are more like us, and this often goes way beyond the conscious into the unconscious. By "copying" or matching your behaviors, regarding cadence, body language, patterns of language, etc. you will find that it is easier to build up a rapport with them and easier to persuade them to your way of thinking.

14. Be Flexible in Your Behavior

Have you considered why children are often so much more persuasive than adults are? It's because they are quite happy to work their way through a whole list of behaviors to get what they want – crying, being charming, pleading, trying to strike bargains, etc. Parent are stuck with just one response – No – which often turns to another – Yes.

The more different behaviors you have in your repertoire, the more likely you are to be persuasive.

15. Be Detached and Calm

If you are in a situation where emotion is running high, you will always be the most persuasive person if you are calm, show little to no emotion and remain detached from the situation. In times of conflict, people will turn to you for help, and they will trust you to lead them in the right direction.

16. Use Anger in the Right Way

Most people really don't like conflict and if you are prepared to escalate a situation to a level of high tension and conflict, many of your adversaries will back down. Don't make a habit of doing this and never do it when you are in an emotional state or are on the verge of losing control. Do use anger in the right way to gain the advantage.

17. Be Confident, Be Certain

The most intoxicating and compelling quality is certainty. If you are confident and full of certainty, you will have the edge in persuading people to follow you.

Believe in what you do, believe in what you say and you will always be able to persuade the next person to do what is right for them and to benefit you as well.

Chapter 1: The Art of Persuasion

Historically, persuasion is rooted in ancient Greek's model of a prised politician and orator.

To make the list, a politician or orator needs to master the use of rhetoric and elocution in other to persuade the public. Rhetoric, according to Aristotle, is the "ability to make use of the available methods of persuasion" in order to win a court case or influence the public during important orations. On the other hand, elocution (a branch of rhetoric), is the art of speech delivery which may include proper diction, proper gestures, stance and dress. Although Grecian politics and orations seem clearly to be the genesis of persuasion, its use in the rapidly developing world of the twenty-first century goes beyond politics, oration and other human endeavors.

Persuasion, in the business domain, refers to a corporate system of influence aimed at changing another people, groups, or organizations' attitude, behavior or perception about an idea, object, goods, services or people.

It often employs verbal communications (both written and spoken words), non-verbal communication (paralinguistic, chronemics, proxemics and so on), visual communication or a multimodal communication in order to convey, change or reinforce a piece of existing information or reasoning peculiar to the audience. Persuasion in business can come in different forms depending on the need of the management. For instance, business enterprise sometimes uses persuasion in cases like; public relations, broadcast, media relations, speech writing, social media, customer-client relations, employee communication, brand management and so on.

Persuasion, in psychological parlance, refers to the use of an obtainable understanding of the social, behavioral, or cognitive principles in psychology to influence the attitude, cognition, behavior or belief system of a person, group or organization. It is also seen as a process by which the attitude and behavior of a person are influenced without any form of coercion but through the simple means of communication. For instance, when a child begs his mother for candy and the mother refuses but instead proffers a better food for the child to eat while also encouraging him that it will make him grow bigger.

The child gets excited and goes for the new alternative. In this way, the mother has been able to tap into his belief system without any form of duress. Hence, persuasion can also be used as a method of social control.

In the world of politics and governing today, persuasion still retains its role as one of the important means of influencing the behavior, feelings and commitment of the populace through the power of mass media. For instance, politicians sometimes use social media, television, radio, newspaper, magazine to persuade the populace to sponsor their political campaigns. Persuasion in modern politics is also observed through the use of authority in such situations where opponents of one political party influence on cross carpet to the other party with different promises in the form of power and immunity. In addition, the court still entertains the use of persuasion during the prosecution or defense of an accused.

Another way to see persuasion is through the intentional use of the means of communication as a tool of conviction to change attitudes regarding an issue by transferring messages in a free choice atmosphere.

The verbal, non-verbal and visual forms of communication are manipulated just for the sole purpose of persuading an individual, group, or organization. Although communication is the most important and versatile form in which persuasion is manifested, it is worthy of note that not all forms of communication are intended to persuade. For instance, the celebration of a newly inaugurated president or governor circulated on the news cannot be classified as persuasion unless it is intended to impact something on the citizen of the country or react in certain ways.

We go further to look at other possible definition of persuasion in the circular world.

Persuasion is a concept of influence that attempts to change a person's attitudes, intentions, motivations, beliefs or behaviors. When a child begs his parent for candy and the parent says a big no to him, but the child insists on having candy even while knowing it might not be good for his health, persuasion is beginning to take place. Along the course of all of this, the parent will try to proffer a better food for the child to eat instead of the candy, the child gets excited and goes for the new alternative. In this way, the parent has won a banter of persuasion.

Persuasion on its own is a branch of communication and also popular as a method of social control, so it is worthy of note that not all forms of communication intend to be persuasive. Persuasion is also a process by which the attitude and behaviors of a person are influenced without any harsh treatments by simple means of communication from other people. Other factors can also determine a person's change in behavior or attitude, for example, verbal threats, a person's current psychological state, physical coercion etc.

Having discussed the meanings of persuasion, it can be observed that persuasion extends beyond a specific field as there are an intermingling of ideas from different areas of study. However, communication and psychology seem clearly to be in use in order for persuasion to take place.

While communication provides the model as to how interlocutors in the art of persuasion get messages understood, psychology provides the model for the mental processes during persuasion.

Chapter 2: Persuasion Tools

Below is a brief discussion of methods you can use to persuade someone to take up your ideas.

Questions

The questioning method is used to grasp the attention of your audience. When asked a question in a discussion, people begin to think about the appropriate answer to the question, and they also wonder the reason you asked them that particular question.

However, you ought to be careful and to only ask questions that will add to your discussion because undoubtedly, your audience's minds will waver as they think of the right response to give.

To get the right results, ensure that the questions you ask are short, simple, and logical. Let the questions inspire deeper thinking rather than taking away the audience's attention from your discussion.

Repetition

Repetition serves to incite and improve your brain's retention power. Once something is repeated to you, the odds of it getting stuck to your memory increase. Ensure that the sentences you speak highlight the keywords you want your audience to remember, and make an effort to repeat the most significant sentences or words. Place them strategically, and where possible, have your audience repeat them out loud, or put them down on paper.

Use Simulations

This is an excellent method for convincing strangers because you have not related before, and you cannot say anything about their mental abilities. You cannot also predict how they will react to certain statements, especially when discussing controversial issues. Using simulations creates an analogy by taking out the names of real places, people, and other things that could distract the listener and take his mind away from the subject.

For example, if you want to convince a college dropout to return to school, avoid mentioning places and names that could change the course of your discussion and shift it in an unfavorable direction. Do not mention the names of people that dropped out of school and succeeded like Bill Gates or Mark Zuckerberg. Do not also mention the names of people that dropped out of college and failed. Your aim should be to convince your audience, based on the unique circumstances that getting back in college would be the best decision he can make.

When you stick to the student's unique circumstances, he is likely to reflect on the reasons you gave and find some inspiration to finish his education. Giving examples of what other people did does not help much, what would help him is drawing the inspiration from within when times get difficult, rather from other people's stories. Sure, mentorship is a useful motivator, but the spirit in a man is what keeps him pushing and motivated, not the experiences of others.

Refute the Opinions of Others

Refuting can be difficult for many people, especially for those who hate or fear confrontations. It is also challenging because it requires a person to pay close attention to the opinions the other person has expressed, break it into smaller ideas, and then go about disapproving every one of them. Once you have knocked all of them down, now present your opinion and show how it is the better opinion. It is crucial that you rely on logic and reason throughout this process and present compelling facts that the other person knows about. That way, the other person will see the logic in your ideas and take them up.

As you present your ideas, the most important thing to do is to ensure that you have proof of your opinions. Of course, some beliefs cannot be proven, such as the question of taste (you cannot say you are right for finding an ice cream flavor sweeter than the other), because neither opinion could be wrong. However, in matters where you can provide proof, be sure to provide it.

Facts give the illusion that what you are saying is accurate and irrefutable. Therefore, when trying to convince people to take up your opinion, persuade them that it is a fact, even when it is not. Sadly, sometimes people twist the facts, but this is not something you should be engaging in.

Manipulators convince you that their opinions are better than yours by first getting into your head to see what you already know. Many of them will get you talking, and as you go on and on, they will be collecting information, wanting to see just how much you know.

From there, the manipulator cleverly repeats the facts you just stated back to you, adding in some more details. You will think that you are adding to your knowledge, but the truth is that these facts may not even be real. The manipulator might be making them up or twisting information to favor them. You see, there are very many ways to manipulate information. Some people, instead of agreeing with what you know, will go the other way and begin to discrediting what you know by presenting it as faulty. They do this by bending the facts a bit or presenting new crafted facts to the table. You end up denying the truth you already knew and taking up erroneous information. By the time you realize it, the person will have gotten away with much.

Chapter 3: Persuasive Speaking

Some form of persuasion is non-verbal. But most people persuade verbally. Being a good speaker is mandatory if you want to be an effective persuader. So much of our negotiations are verbal, and being able to say things the right way will go a long way toward convincing someone to do or think what you want them to.

That being said, most of the techniques involved in effective speaking are non-verbal. To cite the cliché, it's not so much about what you say as to how you say it. There are eight basic elements of effective speaking, and only one of them is actually about the words you use. The elements of effective speaking are gentle eye contact, facial expression, warm tone of voice, expressive gestures, relaxed disposition, speaking slowly, keeping it simple, and using the right words. If you do nothing but master these eight elements, you will see your powers of persuasion skyrocket.

Gentle Eye Contact

Entire books have been written about the importance of eye contact in communication and for a good reason. Eye contact is incredibly important and goes a long way in establishing a connection with other people. The thing you want to be mindful of is what kind of connection you are establishing.

First, not making or even avoiding eye contact can be subconsciously read by your target as discomfort or nervousness. "Eye-blocking" is the process of closing, shielding, narrowing, or averting the eyes to indicate when we feel threatened or don't like what we see (Navarro, 2008).

On the other hand, too much eye contact or "hard" eye contact can be perceived as aggressive, uncomfortable, or even creepy. The trick is to hit a safe balance with your target. Make eye contact, but make it gentle. Don't stare them down; make eye contact that feels easy and natural.

Gentle eye contact will make you seem incredibly magnetic to your target.

Not only will it make them feel relaxed around you, but it will make them feel connected to you, and subsequently, more receptive to what you're saying to them.

If and when you do make eye contact with your target, it's usually best to let them be the one to break contact with you. If you are constantly making eye contact and then looking away, you run the risk of seeming nervous, and therefore making your target feel suspicious, threatened, or agitated.

However, if you seem like you are going out of your way to maintaining eye contact, it can start to feel creepy or invasive, and therefore make your target feel suspicious, threatened, or agitated. If eye contact starts to feel uncomfortable, break it off, but do so in a slow, natural way.

Kind Facial Expression

If you're a top-level sales executive or a CEO looking for some tough negotiating tactics, you might see the word kind and roll your eyes. Kind? Whoever won a negotiation with kindness?

Well, a lot of people. If you're a politician negotiating with a hostile foreign power or law enforcement trying to persuade a terrorist not to kill his hostages, kind is probably the farthest thing from your mind.

You aren't in this situation to make friends, you may argue, you're there to persuade the other person to do what you want.

In these, and other persuasive situations, it's true that you're not trying to make friends. But if you come across as a friend rather than a foe, you are far more likely to persuade your target to do what you want them to do. Put, if you can lower your target's defenses and get them to relax, they will be far more willing to listen to you.

No matter how calm, reasonable, or soothing your voice is, if your facial expression is tense, closed, or hostile, then your target won't be able to relax, and you will have a much more difficult time persuading them. A kind facial expression, on the other hand, will disarm your target.

What you are trying to exude with gentle eye contact and a kind facial expression is warmth. When talking about personal presence, warmth is how we show our goodwill toward others without having to utter a single word. When people are warm, we believe that they will use whatever power they have to benefit us.

If we perceive someone to be warm, we see them as benevolent, altruistic, and caring. We believe that they are here to impact our world positively. And if we believe all this, then we are far more comfortable entrusting them with our decision making faculties. We are more likely to believe them, trust them, and therefore, to be influenced by them. So whether you're persuading your three-year-old son to go to bed or a violent criminal to hand over his captives, successfully conveying warmth to your target will go a long way toward persuading them to listen to you. Contrary to cultural beliefs, perception of warmth is even more influential than the perception of power, because warmth is evaluated more directly by the subconscious than power (Cabane, 2008).

So when you are sitting across the conference table with the head of a rival department, don't try to intimidate him. Instead, try to disarm him. Make gentle eye contact when speaking with him. Relax your face, and cultivate an expression that exudes kindness, benevolence, and warmth. Release any tension in your facial muscles, especially around your mouth and lips. Maintain this relaxation even when he's talking to you.

The idea is to persuade him, even subconsciously, that whatever you want him to do is in his best interests, and that you have only the kindest of intentions.

Warm Tone of Voice

Effective speaking isn't just about the words you choose - the tone you choose is just as important, sometimes even more so. A harsh, threatening, or pushy tone of voice will alienate your target and raise their subconscious defenses. Speaking in a monotone or a mumble won't alienate your target, but it will put her to sleep, which probably isn't what you want either.

A warm tone of voice is the best for enticing someone to listen to you. Whether it's a speech, a negotiation, or a conversation with your boyfriend, you want the other person to want to listen to you, and a warm tone of voice is an easy way to make that happen.

If you're not sure what a "warm" tone of voice sounds like, think about what a late-night radio DJ sounds like (if you've never listened to a late-night radio DJ, go ahead and find one to listen to tonight). No matter the topic, late-night radio DJ sounds calm and soothing.

You may tell yourself you're only going to listen for ten minutes, and an hour later you find yourself still listening. You want to listen to late-night radio DJ, and that's because he has a warm tone of voice. That kind of soothing, comforting cadence is exactly what you want to bring into any and every persuasive situation because it will lull the other person into listening to you what you have to say.

For a more modern example of the warm tone of voice, listen to a podcast. Most podcast hosts (at least the ones that are most successful) also have a warm, soothing tone of voice. Podcasts can cover some very serious and heavy topics, so if you're skeptical as to how the warm tone of voice can work if you're trying to talk foreign policy or convince your Fox News watching uncle that Barack Obama wasn't all that bad, then listen to how they do it. The voice of a good podcast host should almost wash over you. Podcasters are people you feel like you could listen to forever. You're almost disappointed when the episode is over.

This is the power of a warm tone of voice. When your defenses are down, you stop formulating counterarguments, you stop looking for loopholes in the other person's argument, and you stop checking your watch to see when class is going to end. A warm tone will put your target in a tranquil state of mind, which is the best state of mind as far as listening to what you have to say, remembering what you said in the future, and, most importantly, being influenced by what you have to say.

The warm tone of voice doesn't just make your target feel calmer. To pull off the warm tone of voice, you have to feel calm as well. If you allow your doubts, fears, stress, or desperation to creep into your voice, your target will be able to hear it, and they will be much harder to persuade. By forcing yourself to relax and speak in a warm, calm way, you'll start to feel more confident. Confidence alone can dramatically increase your ability to persuade, so confidence plus a warm tone of voice is a winning combination (Cialdini, 2017).

Expressive Gestures

Sitting or standing perfectly still can make you appear stiff, wooden, and cold to your target audience. The key to effective speaking is warmth, and a rigid, unmoving posture is hardly warm.

A little bit of drama makes sense in a speech, but the same passion might seem a bit ridiculous if you're trying to persuade your neighbor to comply with the neighborhood water ban. However, expressive gestures don't always have to be as dramatic as raising a fist or pounding the pulpit.

Expressive gestures are about conveying emotion and about directing your target's emotions. If you want someone to look at something, point to it. Roll your eyes to show that you think something is frustrating or silly. Smile when you are talking about that you love. These simple gestures will go much further in prompting similar emotions in your target audience than even your words will.

Mark McCormack is an attorney and the founder of one of the first American sports management firms. Law and business are two fields where people find themselves in a lot of tough persuasive positions, and if you can't master the art of speaking, you're not going to get very far. He is famously quoted as having said "all things being equal, people will buy from a friend. All things being not quite so equal, people will still buy from a friend."

In other words, people are far more willing to listen to, support, or work with someone they perceive to be warm, friendly, and caring (Fine, 2003).

Your gestures and even your posture has a lot to do with sending that message. Slouching, crossing your arms, and checking your watch or your phone are all gestures that send signals to your target that you are bored, nervous, or uncomfortable. Keep your shoulders back and having an "open" posture will also make you seem more open to what your clients have to say. Which, paradoxically, makes them a lot more willing to listen to you.

Whatever you do, don't cross your arms. This gesture is almost universally interpreted as hostile or uncomfortable. If you are telling a story, having a conversation, or giving a presentation, "speak with your hands." Slight dramatic or comic hand gestures to accompany what you're saying heighten the "performance" of your presentation, and therefore do a lot to keep your target focused and engaged in what you're saying.

Watch out for nervous ticks as well.

Tapping your foot or your fingers, constantly adjusting your glasses or twirling your hair - these small, repetitive movements are ways that our brain subconsciously releases tension. And no matter how friendly your tone of voice, these small gestures will be registered, consciously or subconsciously, by your target for what they are - signs that you are nervous.

Relaxed Disposition

Remember the principle of social proof. We are all wired to be social mimics. This means that if you look nervous, your target audience will become nervous too. If you are relaxed, your target will relax too.

But a relaxed demeanor is not only important for your target - it's important for you, too. Anxiety causes us to forget things more easily, stutter over our words, and can even manifest physically in nervous movements like pacing or picking at our clothes. The more nervous you are, the more likely you are to forget what you're saying or unintentionally misspeak. Nervous hands do embarrassing things like spill coffee or drop papers. Nervous feet do embarrassing things like trip going up the stairs or bump into the buffet table. The more relaxed you are, the more in control you are, and the more focused you are.

The reason anxiety is so detrimental to effective speaking is because anxiety is essentially a loss of focus. If you are nervous, you aren't thinking about what's happening, you're thinking about what could happen or might happen. And while' you're worried about what might go wrong, some do go wrong because you're not paying attention to what you're doing!

The real trick to a relaxed disposition is to remain firmly focused at the moment. Don't let your mind wander any further than the next slide on your presentation. If you are focused on what you are saying, how you are saying it, and how the target is responding, you will have full control over the situation. You'll be able to adjust to your target's behavior, answer your target's questions, and deliver your message in a way that is clear, effective, and persuasive.

If you spend the entire negotiation worried about losing the deal, you probably will.

That being said, if you spend the entire negotiation hoping or pushing to win the deal, you'll probably still lose. Motivation and planning are great tools for when we are alone in our office looking over the week, but they get in the way of effective speaking and therefore get in the way of effective persuading. Planning and preparation should all be done before the conversation starts. If you're mentally going over your notes while you're in the boardroom, you aren't focused on the conversation, and the people around you will sense that you've mentally withdrawn from the meeting.

Stephen Guise looks at the debilitating effects of in-the-moment motivation in his one push-up challenge. If you wake up in the morning intending to work out for 30 minutes, you'll inevitably find a reason why you can't exercise at all. Why? Because the thought of a 30 workout routine seems so long, and looking at the big picture increases your anxiety, which decreases your self-control. But if you wake up in the morning with the intention of doing one push-up, you'll do it.

And then you'll think, "I could probably do one more. And one more. And one more." And before you know it, you've been working out for 20 minutes (Guise, 2013).

This same strategy can be used during a persuasive conversation to help you relax and stay in the moment. Of course, you need to plan a speech or presentation, but the moment you enter the conference room or step onto the stage, don't think about the entire conversation. Just think of the first slide. And then the next one. And then the next one.

Speaking Slowly

Go back to your favorite podcaster or late-night radio DJ. It's not just their warm tone that makes you want to listen to them - it's the speed at which they talk.

Audience and presenters have a different sense of timing. Stage actors probably know this better than anyone. Because you, the presenter, are so hyper-focused on what you're doing and what is coming next, you perceive time to be moving a lot slower than it is. Your audience, on the other hand, is probably more relaxed than you are, and so perceives your timing a little faster than you do.

What this means is, if you are talking at what you think is a "normal" pace, it probably sounds to your target like you are babbling. This causes you two problems. First, if you're babbling, your target has to concentrate a lot harder on what you're saying and may miss crucial information. That extra concentration will also make it harder for them to relax, and therefore make them less likely to be swayed by your argument. Second, rapid speaking is something we do when we're nervous, and so no matter how confident you may feel, the rapid speech will probably be interpreted by your target as anxiety. And if your target perceives you as being anxious, they are less likely to believe you know what you're talking about. Worse, you may even transfer some of that anxiety over to them, which will shut them down and make them stop listening to what you're saying.

Speaking quickly is also associated with urgency. We babble in emergencies, and we babble when we're angry. So quick speech can also be interpreted as aggression by your target, or at least trigger defensive mechanisms in your target, which is the exact opposite of what you want when you are trying to persuade someone.

So first, take a deep breath and make sure that you are relaxed. Again, if you're anxious, your speech will speed up, sometimes without you even realizing it. When you speak to your target, speak just a beat or two slower than you normally would. You may think you sound strange, or even stupid, but your target won't hear slow and stupid. What they'll hear is what you hear when you're listening to a good podcast or a great late-night radio DJ.

Chapter 4: Basic Knowledge of Mind Control

Mind Control and Brainwashing

Mind control involves manipulation, but the manipulator tries to be friendly to gradually win over the victim while brainwashing is the act of forcibly convincing someone to adopt specific ideas contrary to their beliefs. In brainwashing, coercion and force are typically used. In both cases, Mind control or brainwashing can take place either with or without the victim realizing it, but in most cases, the victims come to the realization of their victimization after mind control, and brainwashing has befallen them.

People can be brainwashed through the following ways: isolation, confrontations on self-esteem, Us vs. Them, Blind Obedience, and Testing.

Isolation

Isolation is the act of separating a person from the world, most notably people close to them so that they solely rely on you as their trusted source of information.

Isolation is a means of brainwashing an individual by bringing them more closely to you than their previously trusted close associates. The victimizer attempts to cut off any possible ties with the victim's close associates such, as family members and friends at times, by even discouraging contacts with them and convincing the victim that they are of no use at all. The manipulators are usually aware that the family members would try to warn the victim by implying that they are in a cult or even some dangerous relationships and so they prevent it. They make their victims feel more loved and cared for with them than with their families. In most cases, isolation is accompanied by changes in behavior such as changing names, dressing in a different manner, changing their way of talking, and designing a different hairstyle. This gradually gives the manipulator total domination over the victim in question.

In this case, the manipulator behaves in a friendly manner towards the victim to earn their trust. They usually befriend the victim, making them feel loved and important members of society. Once the manipulator has succeeded in winning their trust, he/she often tries to distance them from their previous close associates.

The victim's social activities are controlled in terms of who they interact with, where they go and who they see. The manipulator needs you alone, and at your weakest point when you are away from your close family and friends, they break you. Controlling a victim's mind involves the isolation of the victim. This is a clear indication that the manipulator is trying to win your state of mind.

Confrontations on Self-Esteem

The manipulator conflicts with the intended victim on his/her behavior with the aim of lowering their self-esteem and how they picture themselves. They try to convince the victim that their behaviors are better compared to those of the victims. They often utter terms such as, "this is childish, "this is stupid" or even "not this way" which lower the personality of the victim. The victim, therefore, begins to feel embarrassed about who they are and hence makes an attempt to please the manipulator by doing what they want.

Us vs. Them

The "Us vs. Them" initiative is a way used by manipulators to have their victims chooses between them or others forcibly.

The victims only have two choices in this case. Most probably, each choice is accompanied by its consequences. The manipulator makes the situation seem as if the consequences of not choosing them will be disastrous compared to the results of not selecting the other party. The "other party" in this case may refer to any other group but, most probably, the close associates of the victim. The victims, therefore, have no choice but to pledge their loyalty to the manipulator.

Blind Obedience

Blind obedience is the act of following specific set rules to the latter, even if the practices are contrary to one's way of doing things. The manipulator tries to make the victim do as he/she wishes by first making them earn their complete trust. The victim, on the other hand, will do as instructed without even realizing that they are being subjected to mind control. Blind obedience, in many cases, commences the very moment the manipulator gains the complete trust of the victim. The victim, therefore, ends up doing many things, most of which are immoral simply because they were asked to do so. It is most likely that at this point, the victim in question trusts the manipulator so much that he/she doesn't entertain warnings from any concerned individuals. Blind obedience is a total subjection which is more or less the same as a cult. In many cases, manipulators who make victims blindly obey them are usually pathological liars and should never be trusted.

Testing

The manipulator intentionally seeks ideas from the victim, after which he/she deliberately consents to them. This is aimed at raising a sense of victory in the victim. The victim, therefore, feels more secure and comfortable with the manipulator with the impression that the manipulator is the only one that appreciates their efforts. Little do the victims realize that such tests are barely genuine. Such a continuous act by the manipulator leads to the destruction and brainwashing of the victim.

Mind control incidences usually involve teachers or close friends, and the victim believes typically that the manipulator has their best interest at heart. They typically provide private information willingly. The manipulators often control the minds of their victims using different methods.

They do this through isolation, moody behavior, metacommunication, Neuro-linguistic programming, and uncompromising rules.

Moody Behavior

Moody behavior is a scenario whereby a manipulator tries to exercise mind control over someone through their actions. As a result of the change in moods, the victim pours out his/her mind to the manipulator without realizing this as a form of brain control. Just because the manipulator can't get his/her ways, he/she showcases a change in behavior contrary to their normal behavior. It is this act that eventually pushes the target victim to change their actions to please the manipulator. Moody behavior as a means of using mind control against an individual is observed among couples, siblings, or even colleagues.

Metacommunication

Metacommunication implies the giving of clues using nonverbal cues in mind control. Whatever an individual says is way contrary to what the sign language he/she is using means. A proper example of this situation is when a parent intends to send her child on an errand.

The child will probably say yes in obedience to the parent but then not submissively. He/she may shrug the shoulders, which is certainly a clear indication that there is no willingness in this. Such action will communicate a message to the parent, after which she can decide to withdraw the task. The parent has not withdrawn the task because she wanted to but because her child is not comfortable with it. Therefore, in such a case, the parent is the victim while the child is the manipulator. The intended action is ignored by the victim simply because the manipulator has provided a clue through nonverbal cues.

Neuro-Linguistic Programming

Neuro refers to neurology, linguistic relates to language, and so neuro-linguistic programming refers to how the neuro language works. Commonly termed as NLP. NLP can, therefore, be termed as the instilling of thoughts in the unconscious mind of an individual. This can affect the victim's response. The victim will agree to a situation solely for the sake of it and not because he/she understood the complete details. The manipulator uses this as a means of controlling the mind of the victim.

A teacher may introduce a new subject to his students; for example, a French class and being their first day in a French class, the students will take time to grasp the ideas being introduced. At the end of the lesson the teacher may assume that the students understood the lesson yet they actually did not, and most probably he may conclude the lesson by asking "are we together up to this point?" the students will give a "YES" response not because they understood but because at the time the question is asked they are in their unconscious state of mind which is just a goal-getter.

Uncompromising Rules

These are rules and conditions set by a manipulator to control the mind of the victim. These conditions are rules that restrict the behavior of the victim since he/she can only act or speak within limits set. Such rules may include the number of times one has to shower in a day, the language one should speak, the people one should communicate with, the geographical boundaries not to trespass, the time of arrival at home, and even the clothes to be worn among many other restrictions. A person confined to such rules is under obligation to abide by them.

His/her behaviors and state of mind is definitely under control. Such a person is not even entitled to making decisions concerning his/her own life. Uncompromising rules subjects one to more than just mind control. The manipulator has now taken the obligation to think and make decisions for you since you can no longer think for yourself and stand on your own choices.

Mind control can be prevented through the following ways: Gain control over any situation, don't do whatever you feel compelled to do, don't let the dynamite explode before you put it out and be an action taker.

Gain Control over Any Situation

Among the ways of preventing mind control is by having control over the situation in your own hands. At times you must handle the situation without any influence from anyone. Divert the locus of power to your direction so that no one thinks for you or makes your decisions. Every human is obliged to individual rights and freedoms, and therefore nobody is entitled to deprive you of them. There is no relationship tie that restricts decision making to just one of the parties involved.

Face any situation that comes your way with a lot of boldness and confidence so that nobody takes control of your mind. One should realize that some situations need your own opinion and power, and no one else's. It may not be possible to change the situation at large, let's say the economy or even a particular country's rules and regulations, but what is possible and even much interesting is that you can always choose to change things at your personal level. Take control and step up for your liberty before anyone else partakes your role.

Don't Do Whatever You Feel Compelled to Do

Anytime you feel uncomfortable with handling a situation, do not force yourself into it. Just as Adam Smith once mentioned that a free man works more willingly than a forced man, so be it. Never pressurize yourself into something you are not willing to do. At times the pressure may be accompanied by threats of maybe losing your job, but still, you have to stand on your ground. The decision is yours to make and so let no situation or person control your mind. On many occasions, employees have saved their jobs just because they felt like there was no other choice, rather than getting involved in the dirty job they were asked to do. Be that one employee who would rather lose his/her job but maintain a clear conscience. We are our owners, and so whenever something feels wrong, we have the right to keep the distance. We have the power in our hands to do what we can and not do what we cannot. Whatever wrong that we do when we play victims to our manipulators will always haunt us and thus controlling our minds unless we clear our conscience.

Don't Let the Dynamite Explode Before You Put It Out

At times as human beings, we find ourselves in tough situations and decide to ignore them. Before any situation gets out of hand, it is wise to handle it and be done with it rather than putting it off for another day, which eventually will always remain undecided. Just as dynamite explodes, so will the situation in question, and for the effects, they will be destructive. There is no need to stay silent over what has already taken place. Just be bold enough to spell it out, no matter the consequences. Once we ignore a pressing issue, there have to be some things that we can't do because we are compelled by the problem we do not want to talk about.

This takes control of our mind, and in some cases, other parties use it as a tool for blackmail. It is better to face the situation before it gets too late. Sometimes we do not express ourselves because of the fear imposed on us, but it's just okay. Speak out no matter the threats. If you are faced with a situation where you happen to witness a murder incident by chance, and then you decide to stay silent about it. Unfortunately, sometime later, the CCTV footage reveals your presence in the scene, and you get arrested not necessarily because you were the murderer but because you are considered an accomplice to the murder by not having opened up to the authorities on time.

Be an Action Taker

As an individual, you need to be aggressive despite the changes that take place in your life. Take action rather than just sitting back and waiting for nothing in particular. Whenever one door in your life is shut, make an effort to open another one. The closure of one entry does not necessarily imply failure or giving up. Let the closed door not be an obstacle set to control your thinking and behavior. Stand up and own yourself.

Maintain the everyday energy and assure yourself that you can handle the situation. For instance, when you lose your job, take action. Wake up early daily and carry out your daily routines as you try to figure out new ventures. Whenever you fall into any trap, that is just a bare reminder that you need to be extra careful. Be an action taker, and make sure to watch your steps keenly before any action. The situation is always in your hands. If you don't take action, then no one will.

The effects of brainwashing and mind control have mostly affected a considerable percentage of the world's population in recent years. In most cases, the victims are usually not aware of the incidences of brainwashing, and if so, are usually in denial of the fact that they are being used as objects of manipulation. It is wiser to open up to any trusted associate when you become a victim of brainwashing, for it may cause psychological issues if not handled appropriately. It is important to stay alert and be safe away from manipulators because, in most cases, the manipulators come in different unknown ways. Stick to your family members and only to your trusted friends. Better still, free yourself from any situations that might make you vulnerable and seem to be getting out of hand. Kindly stay alert.

Chapter 5: Basic Knowledge of Manipulation

Basics of Manipulation

Getting people to do what you want them to do is the art of manipulation. So how do you make people want to do what they want? You must first know their real desires and reverse engineer it toward the goal that you want to achieve. It is said that the closer you are to the person, the easier it is to manipulate.

The closer you are to the guy, the easier it is to exploit, and yes I have said this twice, very importantly. Thus the best prospects for testing your manipulation skills are romantic partners or friends. And if "manipulation" sounds like a bad word, consider it to be persuasion.

Sun Tzu's Art of War is the perfect book for understanding that. As he says, "We need to know our self and our opponent." You want people to be convinced. You must make people feel that it has been their decision all along. Men generally want perfectionism and women tend to want honesty. What does that mean, then?

Men are usually swayed more readily by superiority and the ego associated with progress. Thus the show of confusion as to whether or not a man can improve taunts the ego in a gentle manner which yields development. Being compatible with women in several areas of life, particularly with friends and family relationships, is a MUST. Therefore, it generates an intense desire to bring it up by suffocating time or effect on real connections. We do need balance on an individual level, and we all need to compromise and concentrate. But compared to the general population, women tend to lean toward equilibrium while men tend to lean toward focusing on perfectionism. Always manipulate for a particular gain, not just because you're bothered. There are many ways to manage. You can control other emotions, for example. If you want something great from somebody, just ask them for something that you don't need, but what the other person wouldn't accept to fulfil. So ask them whatever you want them to do, they feel ashamed of not doing the former, and they are more likely to agree and do so. There are also things like love bombing, playing the victim to make someone feel bad, and so on.

You can't fight it, though, if the manipulator is subtle and beautiful enough, if you detect a trick then just threaten the manipulator with it and if it doesn't end, then cut him out of existence.

Moral Status of Manipulation in our Society

Consider this case: Lara is hoping to do a task, let's say it Y, but instead, Micheal wants her to do task X. Micheal unsuccessfully tried to give Lara reasons to do X instead of Y. When Micheal is reluctant to resort to intimidation or assault, he can use any of the tactics below to try to influence Lara's decision.

- For instance, Micheal could charm Lara by doing X in wanting to please or overstate the benefits of doing X and the downside of doing Y, and understate the drawbacks of doing X and the benefits of doing Y.

- Make Lara feel guilty because she prefers to do Y. Induce Lara into a state of mind that makes X seem more appropriate than it is. Find out that doing Y would make Lara seem less desirable and attractive to her peers.

- Make Lara feel bad about herself and portray Y as a choice that will confirm or exacerbate that feeling, and describe X as a choice that will either disconfirm or combat it.

- Do small favor to Lara before telling her to do X, so she feels compelled to do so. Let Lara doubt her own decision, so she can rely on the advice of Micheal to do X.

- Make it clear to Lara that if she does Y instead of X, Micheal will withdraw his affection, sulk or become irritable and unpleasant in general.

- Reflect on some part of doing Y that Lara fears and ramps up the alarm to get her to change her mind about doing Y.

One can reasonably call each of these techniques a form of coercion. People also have more specific, familiar names such as "guilt trip", "gas lighting", "peer pressure" and emotional blackmailing. Maybe not everyone will agree that any techniques on this list are adequately described as manipulation. And in some situations, whether the method appears deceptive may depend on different details not defined as stated in the case. For instance, if Y is gravely immoral, then it may not be manipulative for Micheal to induce Lara to feel guilty of planning to do Y. It's also possible that we could review our judgments on some of these tactics in the light of a properly worked-out and excellently-supported manipulation theory — if we had one. However, in the present context, this list will provide a reasonably good understanding of what we mean by "manipulation." It should also serve to illustrate the full range of widely defined techniques as exploitation.

The word "manipulation" is commonly thought to include an aspect of moral disapproval: suggesting that Micheal manipulated Lara is widely regarded as an honest critique of the actions of Micheal. Is there always immorality in manipulation? What is unethical coercion (when it is illegal) for? If the pressure is not still wrong, then when it is immoral, what determines? We will discuss in detail about manipulation in daily life, and the final decision will be yours.

Why Manipulate People in Daily Life?

Many people engage in frequent manipulation. For example, telling someone, you feel "good" when you are sad is substantially a form of manipulation because it influences the attitudes and responses of your acquaintance towards you. ofNevertheless, coercion may also have subtler effects and is often related to emotional abuse, especially in intimate relationships. Many people view manipulation negatively, primarily when it affects the manipulated person's physical, emotional, or mental health.

While people who exploit others often do so because they feel the need to dominate their behavior and climate, an instinct often arising phobias and this is not healthy. Trying to manipulate someone may keep the manipulator from relating to his authentic self, and being manipulated may cause an individual to experience a wide range of positive or adverse effects. What makes a person resort to using manipulation tactics to try to achieve the desired goal.

The first explanation-fear is quite clear. The fear that this individual will not get the desired result created from his own merits as things stand. Your life will not provide favorably and other men. That life is placed against this guy and others. This is a belief that others will benefit something they won't, and that in a world of dog eat dogs there are limited resources that need to be safeguarded and managed to survive socially, physically or financially. What's going to be my life if I don't make this happen? And if I don't, someone will overpower me with the upper hand. Now let's dig deeper. The underlying fear manipulation acts stems from a lack of worthiness in an individual. It translates as: I am not worthy of life living for myself, and I am not worthy of life and other people with a heart in my best interests. How a person perceives the relationship between them and life is basically how this person sees himself. So the real belief, to simplify it, is: I'm unworthy.

Daily Life Examples

Nowadays, when we refer to the term manipulation, it's most often a negative connotation that implies control or influence to one's advantage–like a lose-win situation. Nevertheless, it depends entirely on our personal preferences, expectations or perceptions which would make us feel we have been manipulated.

For instance, I would say, my aunt was shaping me to visit her house as she wanted anything from me but used "it's been a long time since we've met" as a statement to initiate the conversation. Those of us who prefer "direct conversations" may describe this as deceptive, but some of us who prefer not to be direct may call it sensitive or considerate or sincere.

I can only assume that someone abused me, while the person in question may not think so. It is a room which is highly subjective. Does it lead to a question-if am I manipulating? Some examples from today's life might be · In the workplace, when you have discussions with a prospective employer regarding compensation. X will describe your proposed annual salary as Total Pay. From the candidate's viewpoint, it could be manipulation as the real net could be assumed to be less when subtracting through X factors, taxation, mandatory savings etc. From the viewpoint of the company, this is the Cost to Company (CTC). At home, one of the partners who usually cooks can say, "Let's go out and buy something," and then suggests, "Since we're out, let's have dinner as well." In reality, it might be hard to say "I'm not in the mood to cook" because of a sense of responsibility being brushed off.

But for the other person, it may come across as coercion. Particularly on a day when they were not in the mood to go out or eat out· Some relatives may keep talking about their health problems or struggles at times and make it sound more significant than it is. The actual need may be attention or acknowledgement, or sympathy· Children can be viewed as manipulators when they figure out who they should go to for what. But some may find it smart· A friend might invite during my working hours for their birthday party and then get angry that I didn't make it. So, there may be many instances like that every day, in every sphere of life, be it at work, with family, with friends that could be considered coercion. But the point is, whether or not, I'd feel manipulated depends on the standards I set. Anyone could see it differently in the same situation.

In a situation where I feel I've been controlled, it helps go beyond the face value and ask questions to clarify instead of staying with that sensation and perceived reality. Sharing our perspective is likewise essential. The act of manipulation could be the deliberate or unintentional-the only way to find out is by opening the communication lines.

We may also have to be cautious sometimes to treat a pathological manipulator, but then could that also make us come across as a manipulator and how much do we care about it? It is for us to make choices.

Chapter 6 Basic Knowledge of Dark Psychology

Dark Psychology is a branch of psychology that fascinates people across the globe who are interested in topics like understanding the criminal mind, better understanding the darker thoughts that control human behavior at all ages, and the conscious actions people take to influence others using psychological manipulation.

At its core, Dark Psychology is the specified study of the more wicked side to human nature: what defines it, how to observe it, where the lines are and how it can be used for both beneficial and nefarious purposes. It covers mild uses like a clever car salesman who continuously has the best sales numbers on his team because he is able to read his customers and build an amiable connection with them based on observations to the severe uses like studying the mind of criminals who use their understanding of human behavior to victimize others.

The bleak title may make some hesitate before trying to understand the subject, but the truth is that many of the elements of Dark Psychology are in use (sometimes intentionally, sometimes unconsciously) in everyone's daily interactions and communications with other people from friends and family to clients or even perfect strangers. We'll be focusing specifically on psychoanalysis for this piece, but for those interested in a more in-depth look at Dark Psychology and its most powerful elements, check out our book, Dark Psychology: The Ultimate Beginner's Guide to Influencing People with Persuasion, Manipulation, Deception & Mind Control.

Chapter 7: How to Persuade People Using Mind Control

Conventional tools used to influence

There are various techniques and tools used to persuade people. The variety of techniques and tools employed to convince people to enable one to adjust persuasion tactics depending on the environment and the target audience. It can be argued that different tactics to influence an audience will vary depending on their age, level of education, place, ethnicity and religious affiliations. Conventional tools refer to widely acceptable methods and techniques to persuade people. These tools are conventional in that they elicit the least ethical protest on their usage. In this chapter, we are going to present the specific tools and techniques used to influence.

Logical persuading

Using this technique, one employs logic to explain what they want or believe in. Using logic to persuade is a fundamental tool to appeal to people. Logical persuading is widely practiced and is effective but it does not work for every person.

In this technique, the influencer makes the target audience appreciate the suggested direction as the most reasonable, efficient and safe. Once the target audience has bought this line, they will in turn act as mini-influencers by recruiting more people to the suggested line of thought. Logical persuading is widely used by political leaders especially when seeking to unseat the incumbent. In conflict resolution, logical persuading as a technique tends to deliver.

Legitimizing

Legitimizing implies appealing to authority. Legitimizing is the least-effective technique to influence. One of the reasons for this technique is ineffective is that it takes attention away from the speaker and grants it to a recognizable authority. For this reason, appealing to authority may appear as an attempt to intimidate the audience.

The second reason for this technique showing ineffectiveness is that it makes the target audience aware of the attempt to manipulate them. Consequently, the audience invokes the defense mechanism against explicit manipulation.

However, legitimizing as a technique will work for most people and can elicit quick compliance especially in the formal settings.

Exchanging

In this context, exchanging techniques entails mediating or trading for cooperation and is most efficient when it is contained. In some circumstances, exchanging or compromise is the best way to persuade an audience. A shrewd influencer will create a perception of a standoff or crisis and offer the audience compromise which elevates the liking for the influencer. The underlying principle of the exchanging as a technique is to enable the participants to feel involved and appreciated rather than be passive participants. In conflict resolution and business negotiation, exchanging as a technique is widely preferred. However, using exchanging techniques should be limited to deserving contexts lest it qualifies as manipulation.

Stating

The technique of stating asserts what you want or believe. It is one of the persuading tools and most sufficient when one is self-confident and states ideas with an imperative tone of voice.

In this technique of influence, one simply makes the audience aware of what he or she wants. In some contexts such as the church and school, this technique of influence works. Concerning power relations, stating as technique works where the target audience has no negotiating power when placed against the influencer. For instance, a principal of a school informing students on the need to keep time and submit homework constitutes an application of the stating technique of influencing. Stating can cause resistance if overused. The resistance to stating, as a technique is that it can create the impression that the rest of the audience is expected to align with the influencer and that they do not have the freedom to differ.

Socializing

The technique of socializing concerns getting to know the other person and being open and friendly. It is about finding common ground. Socializing involves complimenting people and making them feel good about themselves. Socializing is a critical influence on power tools and is widely applicable across different settings. Most politicians employ socializing by reducing themselves to the routine life of their voters which makes them relatable and believable. Ever thought why most political candidates during campaigns freely interact with the common man and even ride bicycles? The reason for this is that they are trying to socialize by appearing open and friendly.

Appealing to the relationship

The technique of appealing to relationship involves cooperating with people that you already know well premised on the length and strength of the actual relationships. The appealing to the relationship as a technique to influence is among the most effective persuasion tools. Creating a relationship enables to create a lasting influence as the participants feel that they owe the influence of cooperation and reciprocation. Think of why teachers invest significant mental energy in helping a connection with students. The reason for investing in a relationship is that the target individual readily accepts the persuasion as he or she imagines that the interaction is mutual and considerate of the welfare of the affected person.

Consulting

Stimulating or engaging people by asking questions constitutes a consulting technique.

The consulting technique requires involving people in the solution or problem. The technique functions well with sharp and self-confident people that have a strong urge to devote ideas. People are likely to cooperate if they are made to feel that they matter and this is the logic behind consulting as a technique to influence. At the school level, the school administration will always involve student leaders even when it is clear that the school administration will not budge even if the student leaders disagree. The practice of involving the target audience helps lower resistance and enhances cooperation.

Building alliance

Alliance building involves creating formations to help impact other people through peer pressure or herd mentality. Even though alliance building is not invoked often, in some circumstances it is the most effective tool. For instance, most political contexts may invoke building alliances as a tool to influence. The other benefit of building alliances is that it allows one to have a sort of backup to the attempts to influence. The members of the alliance that you built will carry the burden of your influence which helps spread the persuasion as well as shield you should the target audience get dissatisfied with your efforts.

Appealing to values

The technique of making an emotional appeal involves invoking what people celebrate, respect and adhere to as a society or community. For instance, spiritual leaders will draw attention to values that build up the specific religion and to which the congregation identifies with. As such, the audience will quickly understand the authority and power wielded by the spiritual leader. A politician will appeal to the dominant religious, cultural and national values that the country identifies with which helps charm the audience. An idealist will make an emotional appeal to the audience to desire the envisioned perfect society. Business leaders may make an emotional appeal by drawing the attention of the audience to environmental degradation and influence the audience to embrace green technology products.

Modeling

In this technique, one behaves in a manner that he or she wants others to behave. Modeling as a means to influence can be accomplished by teaching, coaching, mentoring, and counseling.

The benefit of modeling is that the audience is largely unaware that they are being guided to align with the wishes of the speaker. Leaders, parents, managers, and public figures influence others via modeling all the time. For instance, if your mothers show you how to dress by dressing well then she is setting the example and in the process influencing. On the other hand, you are unknowingly trying to be like your mother not knowing that your mother intentionally sought to influence you.

Controversial influencing tactics

The controversial techniques to influence include avoidance, manipulation, intimidation, and issuing threats. These techniques are treated as negative because they deny the target audience the legitimate right to speak their will. The target audience is forced to adhere to something as opposed to their best interests. Think of your school days, or the experience when you were arrested and locked in a police cell. There are instances where the controversial influence tactics may work such as a prosecutor seeking the cooperation of the accused or where a teacher wants to quickly restore order in the school and prevent chaos.

Controversial influencing tactics should be used in moderation and in extreme circumstances such as averting chaos.

Avoiding

Avoidance entails forcing others to act and in most cases opposed to their best interests by dodging accountability or dispute. In this technique, rather than individual leading others to confront their challenges, he or she selectively approach the issue to elicit the highest level of cooperation. For this reason, avoidance as a technique buries any issue that can disrupt the status quo of society and focuses on what the author finds satisfying. In a way, avoidance is related to appeasing where emotive issues are overlooked and the influencer concentrates on what people desire to hear.

Manipulating

In manipulation, one seeks to influence through deceit, lies, swindles, and hoaxes. Hiding your real intention or deliberately withholding information others need to arrive at the right conclusion is manipulation. In manipulation, the individual seeks to use the masses to accomplish selfish gains at the expense of others. Bullies and tyrants prefer intimidation.

Threatening

Issuing threats lest they comply and making examples of some people so others understand that the threats are real. Issuing threats is widely used by tyrants and dictators. In most cases, threats help attain short-term compliance but in the absence of close supervision, the target individuals quickly let go of the modified behavior and perceptions. Think of your early school days, there are chances that you were issued with threats that made you and others readily comply but as soon as you realized that, you can navigate the consequences the threats no longer counted.

In some cases, managers or supervisors may issue threats, especially where the employees are resisting change. A supervisor may threaten employees that those that do not learn to use the new system may face forced early retirement. In this context, the employees will buy into the recommendations of the supervisor due to the potency of the threats issued.

Sanctions

Through this technique, the individual issues sanctions, which are well-calculated restrictions that create uneasiness on the target.

Sanctions force the affected person to feel emotional, social, personal and economic pressure to which the person blames himself or herself. Sanctions may involve influencer banning or making it difficult for others to transact with you. At the global stage, economic sanctions help exert control over the targeted country. If a country receives sanctions then it is deliberately denied trade partners which elevate negative publicity of the country. A real-life example is how the United States uses sanctions to contain other emerging economic powers that do not cooperate with the United States.

Information control

Filtering information can elevate one over others. Multiple contexts make people desperate for information. It is one reason why media houses wield influence. However, when practicing information control, it is necessary to uphold consistency. The other effect of information control is that it makes the individual be perceived as being connected, knowledgeable and powerful which enhances the influence that he or she wields.

Due to the proliferation of social media, withholding information may not always work as people can still access the much-needed information from independent influencers.

Image management

In this context, image management includes the character, personality, grooming and diction of an individual. Your style and consistency of dressing affect how people perceive you. Additionally, a certain form of dressing may communicate nonconformity or gentleness. Similarly, the choice of words by a person will determine the reception and reaction of the target audience. Our character may make us find it easier or difficult to influence others. Concerning personality, our personality rarely changes compared to character. For this reason, one should define their personality and use the patch up the shortcomings when attempting to influence.

Chapter 8: Persuasion and Manipulation

People always have different ideas of what words mean, but to be successful in manipulation and persuasion, you need to know the different ways these terms are understood as well as what we mean when using them in this book. In common speech, persuasion is considered a neutral word; of course, someone can be persuaded to do something that helps the persuader and not themselves, but the word itself does not imply that. Manipulation, on the other hand, tends to mean ill intention of the manipulator.

The ethics of manipulation and persuasion are a topic we have explored throughout these pages, but know that for our purposes, persuasion is changing someone's beliefs, while manipulation is changing someone's actions. This is easy to remember, because NLP involves the neural pathways for both language (belief) and programming (action).

If you want your subject to change their behavior, you have to get them to change their thinking about their behavior. They are a thinking person just like you are, and while they have mental shortcuts that can get in the way (just like they can for you), your subject is entirely capable of talking through their judgment calls with you. In a conversation with you, they can come to re-evaluate their actions, and if you go through the conversation the right way, you will have the opportunity to convince them to change.

When it comes to manipulation, there is a slight difference from persuasion. The difference is that at some points, it is, in fact, the right thing to ask them to change their behavior directly. Now, you don't want to pull this out as your first move. This is something you build up to after a long conversation — after you accomplish steps zero and one, just as you do for persuasion. But the big difference between changing someone's ideas and changing their behaviors is here in step two: more often than not, you should directly tell them what you think they should do differently.

When NLP newcomers learn this at first, they are totally taken aback. They think, how could I possibly be told to tell them directly to change their behavior? But if you think through it a little longer, it makes sense.

What is the difference between belief and behavior? Persuasion changes belief by getting close to someone's mind and changing what is in there, and manipulation is getting closer to their mind and changing what is in there, too.

But with manipulation, there is the added hurdle of getting them to follow up on the change in thought. While it is absolutely true that all of our behavior ultimately comes from our mind, our brains are still not simple masters of our actions. Rather, our actions are determined by multiple factors other than simply what our brain tells us to do. The reason you eventually have to ask your subject to change their actions directly is that for new behaviors, a change in thought is just not enough.

Your subject needs voices other than the one in their head, telling them what to do. They have the thought you got into their head through NLP; you are telling them directly, too. But there is still more you have to do.

Social bonds are incredibly important to human beings. If you want to manipulate someone's behavior, unlike when you persuade them into having new thoughts, these thoughts alone are not enough. You telling them what to do is not enough, even once they have recognized you as like them. If you want to change their behavior, next, you have to change the social environment of the person with the undesired behavior.

This is not a catch-all for manipulation, because nothing is. After all, not in every situation will you be able to change the social environment of your subject. If they are not friends or family, but rather a co-worker, this could prove much more challenging. It is only fitting since manipulation is a more difficult and complicated task than persuasion.

But if this is a person whose social environment you have some control over, you have to determine what social factors are leading to undesired behaviors. Is there another family member enabling their drinking or drug use? This is the most prominent example, but all of it is emblematic of the NLP manipulation framework in general.

All of this is to say that when you are not in control of a person's social environment, directly telling them what action they should take is a necessary and challenging part of the process.

It is so challenging because there is no way around it, and it is also very easy to do the wrong way.

You have to work hard not to work too hard for them. If they can see how badly you want them to change their behavior, they will want to continue acting the way they do out of spite. Don't give them this opportunity.

Recall how with persuasion, we said never to address objections to your frame. In fact, if at all possible, you don't want to address the frame itself. That's because if you address the frame itself, you are acknowledging the fact that it is not the naturally-occurring reality that you want your subject to see it as. However, with manipulation, the situation is different than it is for persuasion.

With manipulation, you have to respond to objections directly, because you have to tug harder than you do with persuasion. You see, persuasion is a subtler, quieter art than manipulation. This is not to say that manipulation is loud and aggressive, because it is not.

But you can't be quite as gentle with manipulation. You want them to change their habits, so in order to get your subject to understand the gravity of the situation enough to trigger the behavior change, it is necessary that you are slightly pushier than you are with persuasion. Again: don't be pushy, but you can't be as subtle as you are with persuasion.

Even when you deal with their objections, you are better off preparing for them before they come up. When you are ready for any question or complaint your subject can haul at you, it is a signal to them that you are like them, you see things from their side, and perhaps, you know better. This is Step One yet again. If you demonstrate that you are like them and can reason things out better, they will listen. You are almost ready to get into the techniques of manipulation, but before then, you need to get into the personality of the NLP manipulator.

You might think that you are born with a certain personality, and you can't do anything to change it, but this couldn't be further from the truth. In fact, the kind of personality you should adopt to get people to do what you want is one that anyone can learn.

Why is learning this personality so important? Well, it's important because you need to seem like you are positive about what you are saying.

If you seem even a teensy bit unsure in any of your speech or your body language, nobody is going to buy what you are selling. That's why in your body language, dress, facial expression, tone of voice, and words, you need to pull off the personality of someone who knows what they are talking about.

They have the answer to your question; they know what's what. If you can pull off that personality, you basically don't have to do anything else. Personality is everything — don't forget that.

Personality is so important because no matter how unlikely something seems on the surface, if it comes out of the mouth of the right personality, people will believe in it. You have to believe in what you are saying to some extent if you expect to pull this off, so don't think you can playact your way through the whole thing — after all, you are not doing the personality right if you are unsure about the merits of what you are saying. But more important than anything you say is the personality you are displaying while you say it.

Not everyone has this naturally, but it is not nearly as hard to learn as you might think. The right place to start is always your breathing and your posture.

You already know what the right posture to take is — stand up straight and without shaking. Now, take deep breaths like for your state control exercises. Just like before, don't breathe loudly. Breathe deeply but not in a way that anyone can tell is unusual.

The third and final thing you have to do is enter the headspace of this unshakeable personality. Everyone has experienced a moment where everything was going right for them, and that is exactly the place you need to go. Revisit that memory as though you were there again right now, and come back as the person you were in that memory.

The world is at your fingertips just like it was back then, especially if you carry this person inside of you. That person is necessary to succeed in manipulating people's behavior in the techniques coming up, so be sure you have your personality ready before reading. You won't be able to pull these off otherwise.

Chapter 9: Persuasion through Dark Psychology

When people attempt to give meaning to the concept of persuasion, their answers always come in different forms. While some may set their minds on the advertisements and commercials that are everywhere in modern society, urging one to patronize a certain product or service over another, others' minds fall back to the politicians that try to change the minds of voters just to get one more vote at the polls. Both examples are correct as they are messages aimed at changing the perception of the subject.

The point of diversion between normal persuasion and dark persuasion is that dark persuasion does not always have a moral justification. While a normal persuader may try to persuade someone for that person's own good, a dark persuader does so with motivations that aren't always good for the other person. They try to get a full grasp of understanding of the person they wish to persuade, and they take pains to do so because they know what the biggest motivation is.

While persuasion always has moral implications, a dark persuader does not concern themselves with these implications. In fact, they are aware of them but choose to place their eyes on their objective(s) instead.

Persuasion is a psychological phenomenon in the everyday life of a human being. It is either that you are the one trying to persuade someone else or you are being persuaded. What makes the difference between dark and normal is the motivation behind it. In mass media, politics, advertising and legal decisions, persuasion comes into play all the time. The outcome of practicing it in these fields is determined by ways of persuasion which will influence the subject of persuasion.

There are some obvious and very crucial differences between persuasion and other types of mind control such as brainwashing and hypnosis. While these two require that the subject should be isolated in order to change their minds and identity, persuasion does not also require isolation.

In order to get to the goal, manipulation is used on one person. Although persuasion can also be done on a single subject in order to get them to change their minds, there is also a possibility of using it on a large scale to change the minds of a whole group or even an entire society.

For this reason, persuasion be a more effective mind control technique and perhaps more dangerous because it can change the minds of many people at the same time instead of the mind of just one person at a time.

There are several people that make the mistake of thinking they have an immunity to the effects of persuasion because they are of the opinion that they will always be able to see every sales pitch that comes their way. They believe they will always be able to use logic to get a grasp of what is going on and then find a logical conclusion to it.

Thanks to the fact that people are not always going to fall for everything they hear if they use logic, this may be true. It is also possible to avoid persuasion because the argument does not augur well with the person's beliefs no matter the strength of the argument.

However, there are people who know how to use persuasive messages to encourage people to patronize the latest gadgets or products in the market.

This act of persuasion is very subtle so the subject will not always identify it, so it is going to be quite hard for them to always be able to form an opinion about the information they are going to get.

Every time persuasion is mentioned, it is very likely that one thinks of it in a bad light. This is because they tend to automatically think of a conman or salesman who is always trying to get them to change their perspective and who will eventually push them until this change is achieved.

While dark persuasion is prominent in sales and conning practices, there are also ways that persuasion can be used for good, like in diplomatic relations between international bodies or in public service campaigns. The difference only lies in the way the process of persuasion is brought to play.

Dark Persuasion Techniques

When a person is willing to change the mind of their subject by persuading them to do something that is contrary to their initial state of mind, the persuader is going to have some well laid out techniques to help them achieve their goals.

Each day that passes, the target is going to face different types of persuasion. For food makers, their goal will be to get their target to try out their new recipes or have them stick to the old ones, while studios will flash their latest blockbuster movies on the faces of their targets.

Whatever the case may be or whatever product they are selling, their main aim is to make more sales and that is why they are trying to persuade you. They really couldn't care less about how this will impact you and this is the reason why they must be very careful and skilled in the art of subtle persuasion to ensure that they do not tip you off or get you agitated. Since there are also many other brands trying to persuade you, they must find a unique way to impress their views on you.

Due to the influence of persuasion on a wide range of people, the techniques used in it have been a subject of study for many years, dating back to ancient times. This is because influence is a very useful tool in the hands of a wide range of people.

Starting from the early 20th century, the formal study of these techniques began to grow.

Remember that the goal of trying to persuade people is to push a persuasive argument on an audience and have them convinced. They will then internalize this message and adopt it as their new attitude or even way of life. For this reason, there is a great need to discover the most successful persuasion techniques.

There are three dark persuasion techniques that have proven to be of great value over the years. We shall discuss those three in this section

Create a Need

This is one of the most fruitful ways of getting a person to change their point of view or way of life. The person that is trying to persuade a target will either create a need or capitalize on a need that the subject already has. If this is done in a proper way, it has the potential of appealing a great deal to the target.

What this means is that in order to be successful, the persuader must appeal to the needs that are of more importance to the target. This may be their need to fulfil their dreams or of boosting their self-esteem. It may also be their want for love, shelter or food.

This method will always work out well because there is no way the subject is not going to need any of these things, or in need of anything at all for that matter. Since there is no way the target isn't going to have dreams and aspirations, the persuader will only have to find ways to make the victim understand how they can easily help the victim achieve those dreams.

The persuader may also tell their target that the target will realize their dreams if they make certain alterations to their beliefs or perspective. Doing this, according to the persuader, will give the target a higher chance of achieving success.

For example, a young man that wants to get intimate with a lady may tell her that he will help her improve her grades and finally make her parents proud by getting an A, but only if she becomes friends with him. While this lady may think that she has finally found the redemption she needs, the truth is that the young man isn't very interested in how well she performs in school, her academics are only a bait for getting access to sex.

Appealing to Social Needs

The other technique that the persuader can use is identifying the target's social needs. While this may not yield as many results and the target's primary needs will, it is still an important tool in the hands of the persuader.

There are people who are naturally drawn to crowds and desire to be wanted. They always want to have certain items, not because they need them but because it comes with certain prestige that makes them feel as though they belong to a higher class.

The notion of appealing to the target's social needs is what is obtainable through many TV commercials where viewers are encouraged to buy a product so that they will not be "left behind." When they can identify and appeal to the social needs of the target, the result is they are able to reach a new area of the target's interest.

Making Use of Loaded Words and Images

When a person is trying to persuade someone else, they must be careful with their choice of words as words can make all the difference. While there are many ways to say a thing, one way of saying it may be more potent than the other.

When it has to do with persuasion, one of the most important things is knowing how to say the right thing at the right time. Words are always the most important tools in communication and knowing the right call-to-action words.

Dark persuasion is one of the most powerful concepts of dark psychology, but sadly it is always overlooked and underestimated. This may be because, unlike the other methods of mind control, persuasion leaves the target with a choice. In the other mind control methods, the target is forced into submission and sometimes this is done by putting them in isolation so that at the end, they do not have any say in the outcome of the process.

When it comes to persuasion, the chips are laid bare (although with an ulterior motive in dark persuasion) so that the target is left to make the decision that they think will suit them best.

Chapter 10: How to Obtain what you Want

For some people, the art of persuasion comes easily. You can watch them talk to almost anyone, and it seems like they will always get the response that they want from the other person. On the other hand, there are those people who may have the best message in the world who couldn't convince anyone, even their closest friends, to do something. No matter where you fall in either of these groups though, with a little bit of practice and hard work, you will be able to learn how to use persuasion to your advantage.

In terms of the process of using persuasion, there will usually be three parts that you need to follow including:

The communicator, or the medium used as the source of persuasion

The persuasive nature of the appeal

The audience or the target person that the appeal is going to be sent too.

Each of these elements needs to be accounted for before you try to use persuasion on a higher level. It is always a good practice to look around you and check to see how many instances of persuasion are going on in your daily life. Some of these are going to be overt, but many of them are going to be pretty subtle. This can be great training for persuasion because you will be able to employ the same kind of tactics. Let's take a look at some of the options that you can use when it comes to good persuasion and using the right techniques.

Using the Aristotelian appeals

So, the first option that we are going to look at is the Aristotelian appeals. Aristotle is well-known and is actually one of the most famous persuaders of all time. He believed that there were three main ways that a person could approach thing when they were trying to use persuasion to change the opinion of the other person.

Ethos

The first appeal that one could use was ethos, which is going to focus on things such as trust, integrity, and character.

This appeal is going to focus on the reputation of the person and some of the things that they may have done in the past, or even how others think about them today. There are many people who value their reputations, and they will work hard to maintain them, especially if the person is in a high office or in the public eye. This is not a bad thing to care about your reputation.

As the persuader, it is fine to show off some character because this shows that you are a human like everyone else and you can even show off some of the flaws that you have. The trick here is that you need to only show off flaws that are pretty small, ones that the target audience will not see as a big deal, but they do need to be large enough that they show that you are still a person who has some good values and even virtues.

You need to be credible as well if you would like to be persuasive. People are much more likely to believe what you are saying if you are seen as a credible person, someone who is seen as an expert in their chosen field.

If you would like to get started with persuading other people to act in a specific way, then you need to start cultivating the right impression with good virtues, small flaws, and by showing that you are an expert in your field.

Pathos

The second appeal that you should work on is pathos, which is when you evoke the emotions of the other person. You will want to find some way to excise the other person, to get their interest in some way. This can often be done with storytelling or even by referencing situations where injustices were done at some point. You can add in some ethos to this by condemning these actions and describing how your values fall into the matter.

If you are working on this appeal, it is important to use the right linguistics. Language is going to be your most important tool for getting the emotions involved. A good speaker will always be able to pick out the right words to get their message out there. For example, they know how to use words that will amplify or subdue the situation based on the results that you want to get.

This can be hard to learn in the beginning, especially if you do not consider yourself to be that great of a speaker. But the next time that there is a big pollical debate or speech going on take the time to listen to the words that they are using. This will help you to see how the words can bring out the right emotions that the communicator is looking for.

Logos

And the third appeal that you can use when it comes to persuasion is logos. This is when you are going to use logic, rational explanations, and even evidence to help support your claims. Some people do not respond that well to the emotional side, and they may feel that anyone who is using their values and integrity are only doing so to make a sale. These people are probably going to do the best with logos, being told logical information that they can look up on their own to verify before they make a decision.

This does not mean that you cannot go through and make some changes to the wording and try to convince these people still. You can always bring the most prominent features to light, or if you know the person, at least bring out the features that are going to appeal to them the most. This is not a license to lie to them about the things that you are doing and saying, but it doesn't hurt to show your argument in the best possible light.

Foot in the door

We talked about this one a bit earlier, but it can be one of the most effective persuasion techniques that are out there. This one allows you to ask for a bigger favor after you have already been granted a smaller favor, especially if they are related in some way. You may start off with something that is pretty small, such as just borrowing a cup of sugar from your neighbor. Your neighbor will probably be fine with this because it's not that big of a deal and most people, as long as they have it on hand, will have a cup of sugar to share with you.

Now that you have asked for that cup of sugar, you may take it up a notch. You may then ask if they have some butter and eggs that you can borrow as well. Since they have already lent you some sugar, they figure it is not a big deal to lend you some more things a well. And the persuader can just keep going, perhaps asking if the target would mind baking the whole cake for them in the end.

If the persuader had started out with asking the neighbor to make the cake, it is unlikely that the neighbor would have agreed. The neighbor might say that they are busy or that they really do not know how to make a cake that well. But since the persuader started out with something small, something that would be silly not to help out with, and then slowly built up from there, the neighbor may eventually feel a sense of obligation to get the work done at this point.

This method can be used in many different persuasion circumstances. The trick is to always start out with something small, something that you think the target will be willing to help you out with. Then you will slowly build yourself up until you get to the bigger thing that you would like them to have in the long run. You may have wanted the target to start with the bigger thing, but if you went there first, you would have completely missed out on the sale.

Reversal tagging

Another option that you can use is known as reversal tagging. This is a trick that uses simple and subtle sentence phrasing to get an agreement, or at least compliance, from the target in general. I t is going to use two opposing structures inside the sentence, the first part being an affirmative statement and the second one will be a tag question.

The premise here is that you will make the initial statement to open the line of questioning, but you will add on the tag question so that the target has a binary choice for answering. This will help you to reframe the response so that it sounds like they agree with you the whole time.

For example, you may say something like "You like this house, don't you?" to your spouse. There are a few ways that they can choose to respond to this. If they say "Yes, I like this place" you would respond something like "As I thought, you like this place." On the other hand, if they give you a different response, such as "No, I don't like this place," you can simply turn it around and say "As I thought, you don't like this place."

Statements like the one above are designed to have a negative reversal element to them. If you do them in the proper manner, the statement will hide the command because it becomes a rhetorical question because it will first tell the person what they should be thinking, but then it inserts the question that will offer a level of disagreement, even though it implies that the disagreement is not wanted.

The key to this method is to ensure that the first statement is pretty strong because it is going to be the main persuasive component. This kind of technique is also useful when you are trying to convince the other person to take an action on something, rather than just agreeing with you. It is the same principle, but this time you will state out your negative first before taking a long pause and then adding in the tag question. For example, you could say something like "You aren't able to do that…. Are you?" this implies that the person is not able to do something and it is going to evoke them to respond in a way that will prove you wrong.

Reverse psychology

This is something that you have probably heard about in the past because it is a psychological tactic that is often used when you want to get the other person to take an action. However, if you are not good at performing this tactic, it is going to seem pretty obvious, and it will not work the way that you would like it to.

This tactic is basically going to get somebody to do what you would like by suggesting that they do the opposite in the beginning. It is going to be the most effective if you can evoke an emotional response because it will stop the person from thinking rationally through their decision.

This is a principle that can work well with those who like to have control, such as rebellious people or those who just like to do the opposite of what they are told to do. It is often called reactance theory, and it will describe the scenario where a person feels like they are losing control of things and they are going to try to grab that control back by doing the exact opposite of what they have been asked, even if it is not their best interest to do so.

Cognitive dissonance

Have you ever been in a situation where you know that something seems a bit off about it, but you cannot figure out why it doesn't feel right? When there isn't something quite right about a situation, it is going o set off some dissonance in the mind and will trigger the person to try to make it all right.

People who have OCD will often know this feeling because they will notice when little things are out of the normal.

If you can change things up a little bit, you may be able to convince the other person to act in the way that you would like. They may feel that their reputation is falling a little bit, that they are missing out on something, or so much else. You can then step in to offer them a solution, an easy to way to change things back to normal, and they are more likely to jump right at it.

Counter-attitudinal advocacy

It is pretty common for people to state a view on something, or even to support an opinion, even if that is not something that they really believe themselves. This isn't necessarily that deceptive because the things that people choose to do this with are usually small or they have the best intentions. For example, it is common for someone to tell a little white lie because it will help to protect the feelings of someone else. When this happens, we are attempting to reduce the dissonance that we caused by saying that our actions are still noble.

Whether you think that telling a little white lie or doing something similar is acceptable or that you think honesty is the best option is irrelevant because you can still use this human tendency to your advantage when you are persuading others. This is a common technique to use when it comes to cults or even gangs when they are trying to change the beliefs of others to justify their behavior.

When you are using this as a persuasion principle, you are going to be tied in with what is known as incremental escalating requests. What this one means is that you are going to offer the target with some small rewards so that they are not really going to attribute this new behavior to some changes. Over time though, the effect is going to keep escalating until it reaches a point where they are doing something that is really different compared to where the behavior started.

A good way to practice this is by getting those you know to go along with you on some small points, but these small points need to have an eventual goal of persuasion that you would like to accomplish. These points need to all be small enough that the internal justification for agreeing with you is not that big of a deal and the other person is not going to resist you or have a lot of questions in the process. Over time, if you have done this properly, the beliefs of the other people should change to fit with yours.

Perceived self-interest

If you ask anyone, they often believe that they are generous and pretty caring creatures. No matter how much most people believe this though, as humans we are really a self-serving species. There have been a lot of studies done on this over the years, and it has been proven over and over again. Even altruism is a self-serving act because it does help the grantor to feel good about themselves in the process.

The idea behind this technique is a pretty simple one to work with, but you will be spending your time on perception. If you can convince your target that they are doing something that is in their best interest, whether that is true or not, then the target is much more likely to go along with the whole thing.

This can be really apparent when you are trying to persuade someone who is higher up than you.

For example, you may work with your boss, and you can say something like "I see my job as making you more successful." This can help to endear a new employee to their boss because even if you are getting some of the credit along the way, you are showing that the majority of the limelight is going to go to your boss along the way, and their self-interest is really going to like this.

This one is known as disrupt-then-reframe, and it is similar to offer biasing and Russian front. The idea with this one is to put out a statement that is completely far away from the ideals and belief of the target right from the beginning. This is like making an offer to the other person that they are not really likely to accept. After they have rejected your offer, you are going to do a follow up that is more rational, something that your target is more likely to go along with, especially since they are still comparing it to your first offer in their heads. Of course, the second suggestion that you make is usually going to be the one that you wanted to persuade the target to in the first place.

It is similar to reverse tagging, but it is going to include a longer statement.

The aim here is to disrupt the other person is thinking and then show them that you can still be rational in the process and that you want to work with them to a better goal. Since you are working with them, and the second request is not so ridiculous compared to the first one that you made, the target is much more likely to go along with what you are suggesting.

Chapter 11: Handling the Difficult Folk

We've stated how you can't convince everyone, but you'll find some people do require a little more work than others. Sometimes, it's because of a faulty tactic you've applied; sometimes others are just difficult. Bosses tend to be a difficult target to persuade in many instances. They're the authority figure in the relationship and schmoozing them to your opinion requires work. Likewise, you can have difficult customers who have grievances you need to tackle. In such cases, it's vital to know a few extra measures you'll need to take to persuade such individuals.

The key here is to direct your opinion in a way so as not to cause a conflict. Often times you'll have to give a little critique to individuals who are not so receptive to your ideas. If you point out their negativity, you'll only reinforce it. But without pointing it out, your idea won't be listened or accepted. So what's the solution?

If appropriate, simply tell a story and take the person you are trying to persuade out of the situation.

Talking in a third person perspective helps to be more objective and logical. That said, this technique can easily be seen as a critique, and if used without proper skill, you're risking being shunned completely.

A second method you can use is to use your words wisely. Instead of verbalizing how bad a person's action is, you focus on how to make it better. For instance, you see someone litter around you. You can either end up in a conflict by calling them a bad person, or you can simply ask "Hey, how about we throw that trash where it belongs?" A positive message is not only well-received, but it helps you get your desired result without negatively critiquing anyone.

Next, it's important to always be accessible. Persuasion needs to be built, so being accessible to people who can reach out with questions and queries about your proposed ideas is important. It also helps to remind them of what you have proposed and subtly acts as its own form of persuasion. You don't need to verbally do anything until prompted, simply exist in front of the person you wish to persuade.

In a parental setting, it's often positive to concede to your own flaws and mistakes beforehand.

Not only are you extending empathy, but you're also setting a fair structure to build critique from. Humility can be a powerful tool when it is mixed in with confidence, and you shouldn't be afraid to use it to your advantage.

Some situations are inflated from the get-go, and you need solutions, not precautionary methods. Let's say that you have an unsatisfied customer. Start by making sure you understand their grievance. Not just the superficial issue that may be obvious, but the deep underlying issue which makes them feel unheard. Level with them and build a connection before you start persuading them. Instead of patronizing them with "I'm sorry," try empathizing with them. Once your customer has calmed down, you can work towards edging them in the direction you want. That said, don't ever try to give orders or manipulate someone. Instead, ask questions. How?

Dan Pink, a leading expert in negotiations and persuasions, has developed a simple 2- question trick to hop into the right direction. These questions may seem irrational, and that's the point.

They're meant to break away from the usual negative talk and make people stop and think. Let's use the example of a boss trying to get his employee to submit his assignment on time.

First question: "On a scale from one to ten, how ready are you to complete your assignment by tomorrow?" The employee will think here. Even if he hasn't reached the predicted ten-readiness, his boss will get a rated response. Then you ask "What can we do to get it up one level or reach ten?" This way his boss gets to start a conversation with his employee and direct him towards the desired goal, all without creating conflict. It plays into everything you've been taught so far and is an effective means to curb any Negative Nelly that may cross your path.

It's important not to annoy people, and learn to know the difference between hard to get people and those that cannot be convinced at all. This, however, is something you'd need to learn by yourself as you practice using your learned persuasive methods on various types of people.

Chapter 12: How to turn a NO into a YES

Have you ever rented a car and been adamant that you didn't want insurance, but somehow walked out with it anyway? Have you wondered how they got you to believe that you needed something that you didn't want in the first place? There is a sort of power and control within the resounding no. The rental agent already knows that you are going to walk in telling them what you want and don't want. Most people do not want the extra insurance because they have their own insurance and feel like paying extra for more insurance isn't worth it, especially when you probably aren't going to need it. The resounding "no" is so common that it is something salespeople don't even pay attention to anymore. It is an instant reaction that is driven by the fear of getting swindled into doing something that you do not want. So, you walk in already with your mind made up.

However, the rental agent found a way to get you to buy the product still. Think about it, before they even work on your contract, they go outside and walk you around the cars.

During this time, they ask you questions about your trip, what you need it for, and then they start telling you about the amenities of the car – that they carry car seats, and they sell you the coverage based on what appeals to you through the conversation you had. You felt like you had a great conversation with the salesperson, but in reality, they were using the time to prey on you because they know what you will need on this trip you are taking and how what they have to offer will alleviate your stress and/or solve your problem.

When changing your audiences' answer from no to yes, it is about understanding how they make decisions, what appeals to them - by testing the waters – how they remember things, and how they look into the future. Most of the time, people remember important dramatic experiences that turn out badly. The rental agent might ask you if you have car insurance and you tell them that you have what the law requires because you own your car.

This is when they realize that they want to protect their car, but they also want to make you think that they are protecting you from having to pay tons of money out of your pocket.

So, they will tell you that they have rental coverage that covers the car bumper to bumper. It is only $11-$14 a day depending on the car size, and there is no deductible. If anything happens to the car, it will be covered, and you will just walk away without paying a dime. This might sound appealing to the customer, but they still feel like they don't need it. So, they tell the rental agent no again.

This is when the agent moves to a story to sway the customer. The agent tells the customer they understand how they feel. Telling them that they buy the coverage doesn't help. They need to tell them a story that they will remember, a dramatic one, which will sway them to their side. The agent brings up an encounter with a previous customer who felt the same way as the current one. The customer was adamant about not getting the coverage that covered the car and rented the car without it.

Another car ended up hitting them in the parking lot, and they walked back in asking if they could get the coverage. The rental agent had to end the rental contract, and not give them the coverage because it is illegal to sell it after the rental agreement has been made and after an accident. The customer ended up paying for the damages out of their pocket, as well as the life of the rental in the shop, which means they had to pay the amount of the rental up to five days. All because they didn't want to pay an extra $30. Due to this story, the current customer ended up purchasing the coverage that covered the car.

When the agent was telling the story to the new customer, all they remembered was the outcome of the crash in the parking lot. They didn't remember anything else about the story, just that they didn't want to go through what the previous customer went through.

Covert Persuasion can be used in different situations, especially when you are trying to win and bring them over to your side. In customer service, you want them to talk about your competitor and discuss their past experiences because if they were satisfied with that experience, they wouldn't be talking to you. One of the things that you have to do is make sure that you don't scare them away so that they do not want to purchase from you.

Have them tell you a story of a great purchase experience they had.

This helps you from not scaring them off because you are having them remember a fun experience. For instance, if you are a stockbroker and the potential customer is someone who has lost money in the stock market, you will understand why they don't want to risk money again. But isn't that the risk with the stock market? You're not going to make money every time.

The broker has to be careful in this situation, and they cannot guarantee the potential customer or investor that they will not lose money again. That will be a lie, and that will break their trust right there. The broker has to point out that it is a possibility that they would lose money again. However, it is more likely that they will get typical returns with their investment.

Persuasion research is very clear, especially with covert persuasion. The speaker must show the audience both possible outcomes for them to be successful. If the speaker doesn't indicate that the investor might lose money in the stock market, they will continue to be afraid of it and choose not to invest with your brokerage firm.

When you show them that losing money is a possibility, you also show them what else could happen, within reason. If you make it sound too good to be true, the possible investor will feel like they are being manipulated, and they will still choose not to go with your firm's offer. By keeping it realistic, there is a high chance that they will succumb to your persuasions.

Be clear with your message delivery. If the possible investor lost the first half of the game, they need to come in strong during the second half. Never let what happened in the past determine what they could possibly achieve in the future.

The whole idea of persuading people is to take away their fear of saying yes, which is normal. People tend to have a fear of the unknown and how their life will change. If you are trying to help someone quit smoking, the person will resist at first because the fear of deterring from their normal routine is too much for them. To help them overcome this fear, you will have to substitute their current fear with one that is far worse. Basically, you are scaring them beyond their worst fears. For instance, the speaker tells the person that if they continue to keep smoking every day that it is going to cause you to die. Can you imagine your kids and grandkids standing over your casket?

They will remember you the way you looked in that casket. The idea of their family looking over their dead body scares them, especially when it is something that they could have prevented.

This is when the speaker makes the fear less painful by helping them cut down. Tell them to start small by cutting down to half a pack a day this month, then only one every day next month and by the next month, you don't need them anymore. Wouldn't it be great to show your family that you don't need to smoke? Wouldn't it be great to show them how healthy you are?

The speaker used fear to persuade the person to stop smoking and then gave them a set of instructions that will help them with the new decision that they made. The person was able to see how changing their life, and going with what you wanted wasn't hard if they worked at it. They weren't going to be worse off because of the decision, but better.

So, once the speaker can change or is persuaded to do what you want them to do, they should be happy that they listened to you and took your advice – whether it be to change their attitude or behavior or purchase what they are selling.

This is not always the case, though.

There is a principle known as option attachment. Someone has a choice to purchase one of two puppies. Either puppy would be a good pet to her, but each one is different. They ponder which puppy they could see themselves keeping, and no matter which one they choose, even though they are not aware of it, they worry that the other puppy will be the better of the two because the person did not choose them.

Wouldn't they feel good about the choice they made? You would think that they would be happy, relieved or even comfortable with their decision. Yet, they are miserable. They start to question the decision that they made.

When someone is left thinking about their options too long, they tend to think that whatever they choose, they are losing something by not choosing the other thing. The initial problem is the choice they are left with. The person feels a sense of disappointment and loss when they realize that they have to let the other option go.

Persuasion research indicates that it doesn't matter if the person has personally experienced both options set in front of them, or just imagining one. Whatever option they choose, the other one becomes more attractive because they cannot have it.

The second factor of option attachment is the feeling of loss. The person felt attached to the other option when they were deliberating.

There are two ways to help counteract option attachment:

1. Don't let the person feel any sort of attachment to both of the options. You don't want them to feel a sense of loss. So, make sure that they don't have a lot of time to make the decision. Tell them that the decision has to be fast.

2. If you have to give them more than one option, make the better option more attractive to them so that they do not spend a lot of time making a decision. Don't let them feel connected with something they are never going to have. Give them info about the option and then make them understand why it is not feasible.

One of the things that the speaker can do is use the option attachment principle to their advantage. If the person is resisting everything that you are doing to persuade them to your side, you can make them feel attached to what you want them to do, making it an easy decision for them. For instance, going back to the puppy scenario from earlier, the person selling the puppies can tell the prospective owner to take one of the puppy's home, and return it if they don't want it. When the person takes the puppy home, they start to get attached and feel a sense of ownership of it. It is hard to give up that feeling without experiencing loss.

Covert persuasion that works starts with the idea that a person's internal beliefs can change when an outside force triggers a transformation. This is where cause and effect work in the scheme of things, i.e., the crash story from earlier. You tell the person that someone else, like your competitor, bought your product and it immensely increased productivity.

Even though the cause and effect arguments are full of holes, statistical arguments tend to confuse people. They want to make an easy decision and not to have to be challenged with thinking.

This is why it can be so easy to persuade them if it is done right. People tend to fight for their own beliefs, then switch them. That is why winning an argument makes you feel good.

Some tactics can be used to help persuade people to do what you want:

1. Get the person to write things down. This gets them to participate in the sales process, or the current argument or debate. They could write down important information you are giving them, goals for the coming year, what they want in a car or a house, write information on a stock portfolio or even a timeshare package. The key is to get the person to participate in the process.

2. Build a stronger rapport with your situational audience. If they like you enough as a person, they will probably respond to you positively and buy whatever you are selling them. You can do this by sharing a part of yourself with your audience; this builds trust because they start to think that you became vulnerable in front of them, and continuing to open up to show that you two share some of the same interests increases this type of bond.

3. Synchronize with the audience. If you resemble your audience, in appearance or personality, your voice, breathing, posture, etc. People tend to respond to others that look and act like them. They tend to feel more comfortable. Once you are in sync with your audience, you can take the lead. You will know it is working when the other person is mimicking you, as well.

4. Get the audience to move around if your persuasion attempt is not working. It has been proven that motion can bring forth emotion. You can either stand up, walk around the room, take the person out to lunch or coffee. Changing the location and physical position can help change the state of their mind.

5. Induce reciprocity. Building rapport helps you build a foundation of concern, compassion, caring interest, and a desire for your audience's wellbeing is an important way to make them feel like they are building a strong bond with you. When you pace and lead your audience, the process creates a sense of comfort for both of you because you are moving along at their pace. After the rapport is built, you can move on to your presentation.

After using these tactics, it is important to use the right words, questions, and stories to deliver the message you want to tell your subject. Some powerful words that you can use are you, money, save, results, health, easy, love, discovery, proven, new, safety, and guarantee. Ask them questions that help keep you in control of the thought processes of the audience. You have to remember that the other person won't be conscious of your persuasion techniques. They will feel like they are in control of the decisions they make, even if you lead them to the decisions. Once they make these decisions, they become committed to them because they are their choice. This is very important in the art of persuasion. The speaker never wants to just win the sale; they want to win the audience for life (Hogan & Speakman, 2013).

Chapter 13: How to Resist Persuasion

We are indeed human at the end of the day.it is because of this very reason that we get to dwell allot on the opinion of others in everything that we do. We always desire and adore getting validation from others so that we can subconsciously decide whether or not we shall be depressed.in this age of the millennial, the norm has become to just brag about their wealth on social media. A lot of these bragging are often than not the truth. This ultimately leads to one having a loose relationship with reality. Self-deception of this type can dig deep into the human spicy, that a victim of these may one day wake up and realize that their perfect world is only existent within their maids. Depression will closely follow suit. The first step to attempting to defend yourself from persuasion and manipulation is confronting the situation and taking the stance of breaking off any illusions you may have. You will not be able to proceed normally with your life. You have to be wary of the fact that you are in control of your own choices. Then make the conscious choice of seeing things for what they are. .

That deal, which seems too good to be true, could actually be just that... too good to be true. The other thing you should follow is to definitely trust your instincts. There are times that a lie has been told to you in the most skilled way imaginable, that you will end up believing. But you can feel an imbalance on some instinctive level between what should be, what is, and then what is being projected onto you. There may be no physical signs to show that hey, something is wrong, but you feel something is wrong. The next important thing when you ask questions is to listen to the responses. This may sound somewhat unbelievable because you'll listen to the answers. The truth is that our self-disappointment can make us choose the answers we receive. We tell ourselves that we listen, but we only pay attention to the answers we want to hear rather than to the answers we receive. You may have broken the illusions around you, but some of you are still clinging to the comfort of those illusions. The pain of confronting the situation would prevent you from listening to the real answers to your questions. Actual listening requires a certain sense of detachment, but this time around not from reality. You have to get rid of your emotions.

Your detachment from our emotions would lead you to the next step, which would logically process the new information. It can complicate situations more than they already are to act irrationally. It makes your exit strategy so much difficult to let all the emotions simmer and spring to the surface. When you face the truth, the irrational part of you may want you to let it all go hell. Your rightly justified anger can inspire you to take steps to calm your emotions in the short term. But you may come to regret these actions in the long term. I'm not saying that you should deny your emotions; I'm not saying that you do not act on these emotions. First deal with the situations and later deal with your emotions.

Act quickly

It's great that you have come to terms with the reality of things. But defence against these dark manipulative tactics entail so much more. While attempting to defend you from the claws of these manipulators, is often intense and exhilarating at first. This intensity of these emotions may cause one to slowly slide into denial. The more you delay in taking any action is usually what accelerates the onset of this denial, and when it happens, there are high chances that you might relapse and end up getting trapped in the same web. This can be avoided by taking action immediately you realize that someone is trying to manipulate you. This can present itself in the simplest of ways like when informing a close friend of some reality of the particular situation may be all that's needed so set in motion a series of events that will eventually lead to your freedom. You should know that the fabric of illusion is made from tougher material than glass after making the choice to act. The illusion could work its way back into your heart with your emotions in high gear by using fragments of your emotions to fix it. When a liar is caught in a lie, he or she may attempt to recruit others to enforce that lie when they feel that they are no longer holding you. A deceptive partner with whom you have recently broken things off would at this point try to use the other mutual relationships in your life to change your mind. If you want to get out of this unscathed, you will need both your logic and instincts. Although the truth of the situation is that when you discover that you've been lied to consistently, you become emotionally scarred, so the issue of leaving the situation unscathed becomes silent.

Priority should be given, however, to take the route that allows you to leave this toxic situation without harming yourself further. You're all over the place emotionally. Rage, anger, hurt, and deception is the iceberg's tip. But logically, you need to think. Keep your head above the water and warn yourself.

Get help fast

When you're trapped by other people's manipulations, confusion is one of the emotions you'd experience. This helps cloud your rational thinking and leaves you feeling helpless. You might even question the reality of what you are facing at this point. It would lead to denial if you continue to entertain these doubts. You're probably going to want to conclude you've got the whole situation wrong. That you misunderstood some things and came to the wrong conclusion. Such thinking would drive back to the manipulator's arms. Resist the urge to give in by receiving a second opinion. People go to another doctor in a health crisis to get a second opinion. This is to remove any iota of doubt about the first diagnosis that you may have and to affirm the best treatment course for you.

Similarly, getting another person's opinion can help you discern the truth of the situation and what might be your next steps. Just remember, it's better to go to someone who has proved countless times they're interested in your best. The next step is to confront the perpetrator if you have the help you need. For this, I suggest you choose the scene or location. Choose a place you know that gives you the upper hand. On your part, that would require some careful planning. If the perpetrator exists in the cyber world, especially if the person swindled you of your money, you would have to involve the police and the relevant authorities. Do some of your own investigations so as to ascertain the truth. After you face the perpetrator and take the necessary steps to get out of the situation, you must start the healing process quickly.

The scale and gravity to which you were hurt, manipulated or abused do not matter. You must be able to walk past it and wait until you can "heal" your wounds, rather than sitting on your couch and reliving the past. Time would give you enough distance from your experience, but if you learned something from this book, it would be almost never healing for emotional scars.

If you don't do anything about it, an unhealthy scab could form over the wound, which would make you as vulnerable if not more than you had experienced. Speak to a counsellor, attend therapy, and take an active part in facilitating the healing process, whatever you choose to do. It won't happen overnight, but you are sure that you get closer to improving every day and every step you take in therapy.

Trust your instincts

While your brain interprets signals based on facts, logic, and sometimes experience, your heart works in the opposite direction by screening information through an emotional filter. The only thing that picks up vibrations is your gut instinct, which neither the heart nor the brain can pick on. And if you can groom to the point where you recognize your inner voice and are trained to react to it, you will lower your chances of being seduced by people trying to work on you with their manipulative will. To begin with, it's hard to recognize this voice. And that's because we allowed voices of doubt, self-discrimination as well as the critics ' loud voices within and without drowning out our authentic voice over the course of our lives.

Your survival depends on this voice or instinct. So, trust that when it kicks in, your brain neurons can still process things in your immediate vicinity.

Some people call it intuition, and some refer to it as instinct, especially when it comes to relationships, they are undoubtedly the same thing. You must accept that it may not always make logical sense to start trusting your instincts. If you've ever been in the middle of doing something and experienced the feeling of being watched all of a sudden, then you know what I mean. You don't have eyes at the back of your head, there's no one else with you in the room, but you get the tiny shiver running down your spine and the "sudden knowledge" you're watching. That's what I'm talking about. The first step to connect with your instinct is to decode your mind with the voices you've let in.

With meditation, you can do this. Forget the chatter of "he said, she said." Concentrate on your center. You are the voice you know. Next, be careful about your thoughts. Don't just throw away the eclectic monologs in your head. Rather go with the thoughts flow.

Why do you think of a certain person in some way? How do you feel so deeply about this person, even if you only knew each other for a few days? What's that nagging feeling about this other person that you have? You get more tuned to your intuition as you explore your thoughts and understand when your instincts kick and how to react to it. You may need to learn to take a step back to pause and think if you are the kind of person who prefers to make spur decisions at the moment. This moment in which you pause gives you the opportunity to really reflect on your decisions and evaluate them. The next part is a hard part and it couldn't be followed by many people. Unfortunately, you can't skip or navigate around this step. This part has to do with trust. You need to be open to the idea of trusting yourself and trusting others to be able to trust your instinct. Your failure to trust others would just make you paranoid, and it's not your instincts that kick when you're paranoid.

It's the fear of you. Fear tends to turn every molehill into a hill. You must let go of your fear, embrace confidence, and let that lead in your new relationships. You are better able to hear the voice inside without the roadblocks put up by fear in your mind.

Finally, your priorities need to be re-evaluated. If your mind is at the forefront of money and material possessions, you may not be able to see the past. Any interaction you have with people would be interpreted as people trying to take advantage of you, and if you dwell on that frequently enough, it will soon become your reality. You know how you attract into your life what you think of. If you're constantly thinking about material wealth, you're only going to attract people who think like you. Using this as a guide, look at all your relationships with this new hindsight; the old, the new, and the perspective. Don't enter a relationship that expects to be played. Be open when you approach them, whether it's a business relationship, a romantic relationship or even a regular acquaintance. You can get the right feedback about them from your intuition. Do not step into this thinking, too, that your gut will tell you to run in the opposite direction when you meet suspect people.

Chapter 14 Learn From Mistakes

In 1958, Rony H. Williams, a U.S. author, and marketing expert said that a smart man is one who makes a mistake and learns from it, never to repeat the mistake. In my opinion, Rony must have been a perfect wise man because reading from my book, repeating mistakes appears to be the order of the day. I keep promising that I will not make a mistake, such as leaving a tap running, only to find that I have done the same thing the next time I turn on a tap. I am confident that I am not alone, and many of us keep repeating our mistakes from time to time.

As you may have realized by now, repeating mistakes can be quite an expensive affair. In my case, it blows the water bill through the roof and makes those living with me unhappy, which is to say that the mistake takes away the joy in my home. Mistakes could cost you the relationships that surround you, cause people to lose faith in you, or cost you grand opportunities like scholarships. The good news, however, is that you can pick up lessons to help you avoid the same trouble in the future.

Below are the ways through which you could learn from your mistakes:

1. Acknowledge the Errors

Most times, when people apologize, they tell others, "I am sorry you feel that way," or "Too bad things did not work out as you had hoped." However, statements like these disguise blame and minimize the individual's contribution to the mistake that happened, and this is not helpful to anyone.

Before you can derive lessons from your mistakes, you must first acknowledge that the mistakes happened and accept the role that you played.

2. Reflect on The Mistakes

Although it may be uncomfortable to dwell on the mistakes, it is important that you reflect on them to understand the situation better. Ask yourself what went wrong, how you should have handled the situation, what you could do to change the results presented with the same circumstances, and the lessons you derived from your experience.

Put down all this information because as you do it, you will gain better clarity of the situation.

You will also think better about what should have been done so that you can come up with better strategies you can use to handle a similar situation.

3. Have A Plan

It is no use dissecting events and drawing lessons from them if you are not going to use the knowledge you gained to help you in the future. The essence of remembering the past is to equip you so that you can handle the circumstances in the future.

Therefore, come up with a plan that will keep you from making similar mistakes. Let the plan be with as much detail as you can. However, be flexible in your mind, knowing that circumstances could change quickly, and you would need to think quickly on your feet.

If you can find an accountability partner to help track your progress, take up his help.

If you can't, use your calendar by marking on it the days by when you should have made certain progress.

4. Put Stronger Barriers

This time, you are going to have to make it harder for you to make mistakes.

Your willpower and your resolve to avoid the mistakes are not enough guardrails because you are likely to go over those when you need instant gratification. You need extra protection to make messing up harder.

For example, if hanging out with a group of people causes you to do the wrong things, try deleting their phone numbers and avoid the route they usually use. If you physically or emotionally abuse your woman whenever you two argue, consider walking out to take a walk whenever a situation gets heated up, and you want to start lashing out.

5. Have Strong Reasons Why You Do Not Desire to Repeat the Mistakes

Your will and desire not to repeat doing something are not enough to keep you from doing something, from indulging in things that you shouldn't. Come up with several fundamental reasons why you need to stay on track even when faced with the hardest temptations.

For example, if you want to stop using drugs to be a good example to your children, carry with you a picture of them everywhere you go so that whenever the urge comes up, you will look at your children and remember the reason for which you must remain sober.

The more you are able to put restrains, the easier it will be for your will to get stronger. Your mental strength will increase.

6. Move Forward with The Knowledge You Have Gained

Use the knowledge you have gained from previous mistakes and practice the self-restraint you have learned in other issues and spheres of life. Use your experience to teach you how to take up good behavior and shun evil habits.

Lessons You Are Likely to Learn from Your Mistakes

After reflection and thinking, here are a number of

lessons you might learn from your mistakes.

1. You Don't Know Everything

People who think that they know everything often make the most grievous mistakes. People call them idiots. Every time you fail to listen to others who are smarter than you or when you know to do better, but you go ahead and do what you ought not to do, you are an idiot.

Idiots need to understand that life is not about impressing others and displaying their huge egos. To be anything in life, you are going to have to work well with others, and doing so will require that you have the right attitude, one that is borne out of being humble. People who refuse to humble themselves, life humbles them, and it often isn't a pretty sight,

2. You Might Not Be as Impressive as You Thought

In life, you will realize that there is someone smarter, stronger, cooler and much better looking than you. I can promise you that.

Therefore, stop going around, thinking that you are the best. Do not compare yourself to other people; be you and work on yourself.

3. No One Is Responsible for Your Happiness

Although people may be taking care of you, they are not responsible for your happiness. Your parents, foster parents, siblings, coworkers and other people in your life are not responsible for you. You are already grown, and you need to take responsibility for who you are, how you feel, and how you turn out. Whenever you are not happy with your life, do something about it rather than pouting and blaming others for how your life is.

4. Avoid the Company of Losers

Some people are not interested in getting the same things you want to get out of life. Some are only living life as it comes, with no particular vision or drive. People like these are losers. They may be good buddies, to some degree, but they are the wrong company to keep. Surround yourself with people who are walking the path you are walking so that you can help each other on the way.

People who do not have a sense of direction will only delay and possibly cut off your progress.

5. It Is More Pleasurable to Go the Long Hard Way

Many people tend to avoid the long way and take short cuts; no many choose to do the hard things. For example, some would rather cheat and swindle others rather than find a job. Others take pills to lose weight rather than work out and improve their diet. These people do not realize that the hard things are the ones that bring more returns to your life. In addition, when you successfully do hard things, it brings a lot of pride and satisfaction to you. It produces a sense of accomplishment that cannot be found when living the easy life.

6. It's More Peaceful to Be Alone

One thing that requires maturity for individuals to realize is that your company alone is enough. You do not need someone else to enjoy yourself and be happy. Of course, you must interact with others in the course of your day, but you must not need them to avoid feeling lonely.

If you cannot bear to be alone, that is a dangerous sign. Time alone gives you time to think and reflect on yourself. It helps to bring out the strong independent person that does not need the opinions and validation of others to live.

7. There Rarely Is Enough Time

When young, in your teens, there seems to be an endless supply of time. You feel that you can do anything, and still, have time to make up for the mistakes you make. However, as you grow older, you realize how limited time is. You realize that there is no time to lose hanging out with the wrong company, working at a job that makes you miserable, postponing your happiness, and doing a whole bunch of things that make you happy. You will want to spend your time more wisely, more productively, doing things that are of benefit to yourself and others.

Conclusion

Whether or not we recognize it, we are exposed to persuasion techniques, and we use persuasion on a regular basis. This may take the form of a high-powered marketing presentation to the wording of a simple, heartfelt love letter. We are bombarded with messages from politicians to leaflets telling us about the latest and greatest pizza deals and no matter how you choose to dress it up; it is all about persuasion. One might argue that the very need for communication grew out of a desire to persuade others.

We have seen that the ability to persuade is one of the most crucial ingredients in our dealings with people, if we are to have any sort of influence and do not want to be relegated to the role of camp follower for the rest of our lives. The greater our ability is to persuade others, the better we will be at whatever field it is we are pursuing, be it social, business or recreational. At first glance, some of the tactics we have looked at may seem manipulative, but when examined in greater depth we soon see that really persuasive people are sensitive to the needs and feelings of others. And in order to remain in roles where they continue to have the greatest influence, they need to be able to generate high levels of loyalty and respect. Doing this requires sensitivity, integrity, and excellent communication skills.

It is not sufficient to simply persuade people to follow you once or twice. To gain influence, we need to establish ourselves as persuasive on an ongoing basis. This requires trust, credibility and a high degree of empathy for the needs of others. Not to mention, practice. We have seen the result of fear generated persuasive techniques used by dictators and despots the world over. In the long term, these tactics always crumble and leave behind deep bitterness and animosity.

The true giants of our society have all been highly persuasive, but yet have not had to resort to fear generating or manipulating techniques to persuade the world to the worthiness of their causes. In many ways, our commonality is greater and more broad reaching than we realize and it is the ability to communicate that common bond that exists between us that separates the great persuaders from the despots.